WE ARE HERE

THE TEACHERS OF THE HIGHER PLANES
First Book of Wisdom

Ruth Lee, *Scribe*

LeeWay
PUBLISHING

LeeWay
PUBLISHING

This book is an updated and revised version of the 2005 edition originally published by AuthorHouse

LeeWay Publishing
Wilmington, DE
www.LeeWayPublishing.com

ISBN: 978-0-9970529-0-9
Library of Congress Control Number: 2015958014
Printed in the United States of America
First Printing 2016

Cover design by Sarah Barrie of Cyanotype.ca
Internal design by David Redondo

More Books by **Ruth Lee**

Dedicated to

Those students whose work is responsible for originally attracting The Teachers to this plane

Introduction

The re-issuance of *The Books of Wisdom* from *The Teachers of the Higher Planes* marks the reopening of LeeWay Publishing, rather than a new venture.

LeeWay Publishing was created to reproduce works channeled by the extraordinary spiritual scribe, Ruth Lee, otherwise known as *The Scribe* throughout this work. She alone supervised the publication of this work in its new format and style, refraining from making any significant changes to the original text.

From its inception, the mission of LeeWay Publishing has been to provide knowledge urgently needed to elevate the consciousness of humankind. As a result, *The Scribe* responded positively to the request of a group of entities from the upper realms known as *The Teachers of the Higher Planes*.

Sent by a higher authority to assist all those who are ready to align their potential and take effective action, *The Teachers* demonstrate ways to heal ourselves, our world, and planet Earth. *The Teachers* provide light in a time of spiritual darkness.

When originally called to work for The Holy Spirit, Ruth Lee had no idea what it might entail. Furthermore, she knew not why she had been selected to scribe for *The Teachers*. To learn more about *The Scribe*, visit Ruth Lee's internet home at www.LeeWayPublishing.com

This material was given in peace and harmony. When *The Teachers* arrived in this world, they had to adjust to the language of *The Scribe* in order to dictate **The Books of Wisdom**. All you have to do is read—then proceed to live a better, more-meaningful life!

We Are Here ~ *The Teachers of the Higher Planes* is not written in arcane language or otherwise difficult to understand prose. It took *The Teachers* and *The Scribe* six hour-long sessions to achieve a style and pace comfortable for all involved. It is hoped **The Books of Wisdom** will provide readers with what they need to know to ascend at the end of this life.

This edition of **We Are Here ~ *The Teachers of the Higher Planes*** begins with their first session. For some it may come on too strong—but you quickly get their message and realize you are now working with powerful entities who understand what needs to be done if we are to be able to depart from this life both inspired and prepared to rise to a higher plane.

Note regarding Chapter One. It was dictated *after* **The Scribe** and *The Teachers* worked together for six sessions in order to align their work and language into a workable and viable program.

In the spring of 2005, *The Teachers* dictated the following Foreword: *"It is not our creed to force you to do something you do* not want to do. We are not college professors or even teachers who usually teach in universities. We are elementary teachers of the universe sent to help each of you, because you have not had much help with ascension in centuries. We are here to teach.

"As time goes by and the work becomes more complex, **The Scribe** is able to handle huge amounts of energy. We have increased the intensity and the ability of **The Scribe** to do this work. You will find that future achievements were dreams when this book was completed (in 1993).

"You can read these books in any sequence and not achieve wisdom, but we still call these efforts: **The Books of Wisdom**. Read each of these books and achieve immortality. Actually, you are already immortal, but some could stay so long in this world that they become immoral, and thus not allowed to achieve a life beyond the one you live now. We would never want that to happen, but you are allowed to fail at life.

"You have free will to do anything you like with this life. However, life is a lot better on the higher planes. Believe us—pass the tests."

The Teachers do not take their mission lightly, and Ruth Lee acting as their scribe, made it her life work to deliver their messages as accurately as possible. Start at the beginning, just as **The Scribe** did, and let their words flow over and through your mind before determining if you can use this material to change or improve your life work.

WE ARE HERE

THE TEACHERS OF THE HIGHER PLANES
First Book of Wisdom

Ruth Lee, *Scribe*

LeeWay
PUBLISHING

Introductory
Session One

All the world awaits the second coming of Christ, but are unaware we are all here! We of God exist in everything you do, and everywhere you are, we are. God is never absent, so how can he come again?

We often hear you speak of second-hand information and second-hand goods, but you never speak of what you know to be true to you—if not anyone else you know who will also talk about such things. All of the so-called facts you have been given about God and angels and such things are in such a tangle of mischief and misinformation it is no wonder you do not know what to believe.

No single individual alive knows how God works on Earth, which is why we are here. Many of us have appeared from time to time to assert God's will and help those stuck hopelessly in time—or what you call time, but we have never been particularly interested in contacting and teaching humans before now.

The Earth is a special classroom where many go for extra credit. It is not an easy assignment. It requires that we sit down with our souls and work out exact lessons on how to develop to a higher level. If the lessons are incomplete, dropped, or failed, the soul has to recover from the loss and return to Earth—and return to Earth—and return to Earth—ad infinitum, until the lessons are learned.

All of Earth is such a mess now that it would take a class of scholars to attend each class and mentor each student to get a passing grade. We are very concerned that the mess is not going to be cleaned up in time for souls to meet their individual *deadlines* (so to speak).

Each soul has a reckoning to make from time-to-time, if that soul is to merge into oneness with God. Now Earth is taking too long to traverse, and people are not learning their lessons. If God should choose, life could be cleared of all foul air and streams in a second, but God lets man dominate this world and try his own hand at management. God is standing aside to see how you do manage it. God is not angry or forbidding, merely sorry sense was so lacking in latest times that anger and greed got to all—even the clearest thinking individual souls have been mired in it.

Now I see you are not as we are. You are not as souls of spirit, but rather as souls of mud and grime who need to be clean before you can be seen. It is not a bad thing to be cleansed, but small children often fear it. We suspect many will hate to be cleansed, but afterward will revel in the wonderment of it all.

Using *I* is a reference to the soul within **The Scribe** and not the souls who write. We do not intend to confuse those who will read these words, but all of us are from many different planes and aspects and have gathered to assemble this work and found a suitable scribe; but *The Scribe* is limited to doing work she can comprehend. Thus, we will continue to use '*we*' when we are speaking, but an occasional '*I*' means we have added her own understanding as well—even though she does not recognize it as being hers.

❧

(You may ask) **Will you hear from souls you knew in another time?**

No, we are not the souls of those gone before you in your place and time. We have never been on Earth, thus are arriving from far distant planes and times. As we proceed to channel this material, and you continue to absorb the truth of this work, all will be made clear.

We knew you would come to this point eventually, and we have been preparing to help you find what you need to know in order to proceed with haste to the next phase of the evolution of man. All of life is a wardroom and not at all a pleasant change from the usual.

We sense you often fear death as a time when you are punished, but that is far from true. You are in fact in the worst of all places while on Earth, and it is for that reason you must work hard to flee it. Work is necessary, but not play! Play is what consumed all your minds in recent years, and those who work hard are regarded as strange and out of adjustment, when actually they are right!

There are three major lessons that must be passed with straight A's before you can go on to another place and time in another plane. The three basic chores that have to be completed by each and every person are:

1. **Work hard each and every day.** There is no sacred day when no spiritual work is required. You may relax at any time, but it is unnecessary to stop your spiritual work while you relax. In fact, that is the best time to meditate.

2. **Socialize with other people.** You must learn to get along with all others who occupy your space and time! You have each taken on different roles from time-to-time in order to truly understand each other, but you must finally assimilate all this knowledge of people and fully tolerate all other humans, before you can be released from this plane forever.

3. **You must do no evil to anyone.** This includes *you*. By evil we mean: physical harm, mental torture, manipulation of others for your own selfish ends. We will go into this more at another time.

These three things are required of each and every soul to transfer out of this plane. If not accomplished, the degree of failure is assessed and recommendations made by the human's entire being (soul) to determine how best to correct that tendency. It may be easily decided within the soul, or it may require the intervention of that soul's *Higher Guides*. If the *Higher Guides* are not in agreement with that soul's plans, an *Over Guide* or judge is appealed to for a decision. At all times, God is the supreme judge and would only be asked for a final decision if all other *courts* (so to speak) have been unable to resolve the issue of how that soul should proceed.

Life goes on and on at the human level, but on other levels—it is! It does not start at one point and progress to another—it is! As a human on Earth prepares to leave this plane for the final time, and is prepared by the soul to advance, this sense of timelessness is *almost understood* once more.

We sense a bit of disturbance in the being of those who fear '*the end*' means the end of all life. They find it impossible to believe this life is not the best of all possible states to be in and thus refuse to go forward. This results in a delay of that soul's progress.

Forget the past! What is the future? All you are and ever will be is now!

In the ways of men, life is seen as a place to assert oneself and dominate others. This is wrong! Never assert yourself over another. You are no better or worse than another—you are much the same; and if you push ahead, you will be pushed behind eventually with the backlash of resentment you started. So leave life to each man and get into the work you were always meant to do—the work you came here to do.

≈

(You may ask) *How do you know what work you should do?*

That is not difficult to know. It simply requires you to remember. Remember the sessions within your soul prior to your entering this Earth plane. The memory trace exists and needs only to be recalled. As you need it and want it, the memory surfaces. But if you refuse to listen to the inner workings of your soul, or you choose to forget why you came to Earth, your entire life may be spent in uselessness. Your life will be dominated by endless cycles of futile endeavors that never meet approval in your own eye. That is the clue to discovering you are not on the right track.

Once a soul discovers life is to be lived according to preordained destinies, and fulfilled by each and every other soul one meets along the way, a unity of peace and helpfulness enters into that sphere and life becomes gentle and loving. We work with all souls, but we love those who love others more than they love themselves. Such a soul is so developed it has no need to hoard its love—rather shares its abundance with all who come in contact with it.

We seek nourishment from the air, and air is now not great, because of such ill will and unhappiness abroad. The very air is made up of vibrations that rise to the highest levels and cause a lot of movement. If the vibrations are stagnant, as they are now, nothing evolves to a high degree at the bottom—where you are. That is why we are here now.

The day is coming when all are ready to be helped. It is not a good time to be on your own. Help is seldom available at out-of-the-way places. We need to be on our own, but you need companionship. If the way grows tangled or you slip, a partner or team can help you get up and over that spot. If you are alone, you may be left to die. That is what has happened.

Each of the souls now on Earth sees itself as alone or nearly alone. We want to shine our light on Earth so you may see how much God loves each of you and that you are of God. You are never alone. We are here.

This is the message for the day, October 6, 1993

Introductory
Session Two

Today is a day unlike any other day, because it is a new and difficult time to be alive. All want what is the other person's, without wishing to work to obtain it. That is the tear in the fabric of your society. You have been groomed to be useless and not worth a lot of respect. In the past all were groomed to change the world and make it better for future generations.

This is the generation all have prepared for! Now look at it! What has been is now being manifested and all is wasted on people who are afraid of God and aware they are unworthy of such help.

We are here to help. God never intended that anyone or other of his people be left to dry in the wind of hopeless endeavor and pain. We say this, because God is here in the words of this scribe. All is in the world. You need only study and remember.

In the world of today and tomorrow, all is ordinary and plain—not pretty. Why settle for such an ordinary world? We can help you paint it in beautiful shades of autumn. The autumn of life is here, and you are only beginning to recognize that fact.

Some still dwell in the summer heat and shade and do little, but some are busy stocking their shelves for the long, cold winter that lies ahead. Winter is not to be feared. It is merely another season of the soul. It is a time when all can see nothing but what they are.

If you were to begin this life again, what else do you think you would need to be a success? A big home and car, a little place of your own, a lot of money, or do you think it was okay the way you had it?

Not everyone had a great beginning, but all are here today. Why dwell on the beginning? Get on with the medium of your life and paint or sculpt its middle and ending. We use the metaphors of art when we describe much of your life happenings, because *The Scribe* understands this. If you were *The Scribe*, the metaphors might be different, and we would not all be the same.

As we write through this woman of Earth, we will often repeat a phrase or two, but not because we cannot remember we said it before, but because it is so important we cannot give up on you and say it only once. If you finally recognize that phrase, then we know you understand. That is what teachers do. We are all teachers of another place and time, as you would say, but we exist now. No more time to be spent on such as we said to you before.

Let us begin with who you are. You are not a being of self—

and anyone who says *self* is the most important being in your life is a liar! You are a selfish impostor if you think you could build a life—good or bad. No one builds a life alone. God is at the center of our existence and lets us build all we want out of clay, but expects us to clean it up and make it acceptable once we are done playing with it.

You will be aware of many things after your time on Earth is gone. You will be able to make it to the top of the world you are in, if you are ready. No need to climb over others—The Top is huge! The Top is not the top of a pyramid. It is a scale of things that need to be accomplished in a grand manner. If you write, The Top is a best seller. If you act, The Top is a starring role. If you sing, The Top is a solo. You get to go forward and stand out alone. That is how you measure The Top.

After the rain of this world is over and flowers bloom and are heavy with fragrance and dew, the nose is a powerful influence; but at harvest, when pollen and chaff are heavy in the air, the nose can hurt your perception of Earth. Never rely on only one of your five senses.

We see you try desperately to develop ESP—as a sixth sense. What does this mean? Are you without a sense of destiny? Are you without a belief that God is the creator of all you know? Why would becoming a seer help you? What is missing from your life now?

All we know is what we know, and you know all you need to know. Why are you going to be better off if you know who is here on Earth beside you? All exist on the same scale. You are not the only one. We want you to understand that if you destroy Earth, you destroy *you*. If you let it go in order to destroy others, you destroy *you*.

We are not here to lecture you on the morality of what you are trying to do to get ahead. We are here to teach you about the implications of your gross misbehavior on *you* and your loved ones of this plane. God never intended for you to destroy anything prepared for your use; however, if you do not know how to destroy, you do not know that what is destroyed cannot be replaced—and that is a lesson.

After a little rest, all go forward again and seek out the light of God in another personality. It is not a secure future. You search for a being that suits you. If that being becomes difficult for you to handle, you can ask to be relieved of that assignment, but it is preferred you stick it out.

People who drop assignments are not revered on Earth or in God's war on Earth. We speak of God's war as a metaphor for what is happening now. You are not at peace. All see themselves as being victims and unable to straighten out their lives. This is a war, so God has to be sure of the facts.

If life here is bad, why do you all want to stay? If it is so much trouble to be human, why not elevate yourself so you never have to come back? What is so bad about Earth?

We are all here to help you seek the right path of life—for *you!* That is not an easy assignment now, but it is not as difficult as you all are trying to make it appear. Let us look at how you look at life, and then we will work on changing your perception.

1. You think it is hard to be good. If it were really hard, why would you still be here?

2. You think you cannot understand one another. If it is so difficult, why do you always want to fall in love?

3. You tell us you are tired of working, but you do not work. Instead, you play and play and play at work.

4. Your work this life is short, yet you think it is long. But in the end, you think life was so short you could not do much.

5. You think your own work is easy and others' work is difficult, thus it is necessary to complain if your work is to be appreciated by others.

6. All of your friends are not as interesting and exciting as you.

7. All of you want to write about yourselves, but you are unsure who you are.

8. If you could, you would be somebody else.

9. The spouse you have, or wish you had, is quickly not good enough once they say they love you.

10. The world would be a better place if only others were more understanding of how it should be run.

Those are a few of our observations. You now can see where we are coming from—we hope. Also, if you are uncomfortable being human, why not suddenly become a changeling and go to another place and time? Stories now abound about the way

God intends Earth to be, and all is so much malarkey.

No way is God interfering now. You are in charge of this mess. Also, you never say God did this for me and God did that for me, instead you say: "I did this. I did that, etc., etc." As soon as the work of your hand is not good, you say, "God let me down. God should have been here to see this didn't happen. God is not as powerful as they say. Etc., etc." We are merely reminding you of the selfish view you have of your life here on Earth.

On the average, you cannot run a business like you run your life. You have to begin to seek help earlier in life. If a youngster asks you for advice, do not admit you do not know. If you do not know, say it is all in the hands of God. Let the youngster learn. Let the youngster sit and listen to stories of worth that indicate life is not easy—but it is fair.

If you work, you can earn. If you steal, you will never accumulate lasting treasure. If it is to be, it will be. Those are very simple, basic lessons anyone can teach. So why aren't you teaching them, too?

As we grow and develop and seek out help on Earth to do God's work, will we be able to count on you to volunteer? Will you want to be on the winning side? Too many act like losers! It is disgusting to watch you plant negative fears in each other's lives. Jealousy is so rampant among you that it is the single worst fear you have today!

Now is not the time to berate you about jealousy. We will do that some other time. Today is the time to speak of fear as the enemy of all. What is it that causes you to be so afraid that you would rather be sick than move forward in the world? Are you still afraid of the dark? What could be so bad that you cannot walk and talk freely?

We seek you out. We do not intimidate you. So why would another human being frighten you?

It is not the right or privilege of anyone to hire another to do their work. If you work for someone else, you are not a slave. The work must be worthy of you or quit. It is that simple! Yet how many work for people who are evil and try to enslave you and prevent you from being free of mind and soul—or try to keep you under their supervision all the days of your life? That is not to be. God does not do that, so why would you give another human being that power?

There is much to think about, and we are tired now. In the future, as our scribe feels better and stronger, we will speak at greater length.

This session conducted on the morning of October 9, 1993

Introductory
Session Three

The world is not worth a lot once all the people are gone. It is just a shell, nevertheless, the people are to be gone. The Earth is not as well preserved as we would like. It has been dug up and ripped open and holes filled with what was once on the surface and not meant to be interred.

We seek the news of workingmen and women and hear them mourn. This is not the time to be without work. The wall of Spirit is descending on the work world and will open up the way things are to be done. If it is not accepted, the world will be placed in a very perilous stage of distance from the wall. We will be here until the world is finished. The world is not a piece of cloth that can be sewn up and cut up again. It is fragile and porous. It is different from any other place.

Food is to be used by others if you have too much. Food is not without double use, but you are aware only of its value in keeping the body together—not the spirit. We are often aware of the lack of sophistication now present throughout the world, and it is most apparent in the way you feed yourselves. The food you eat is not as pretty as it is in the garden. You dully prepare it and eat in a hurry. That is not the way of God.

God intended food to be prepared and eaten as a celebration of the body and spirit.

Love is not gone or even missing from your lives. It is just not outstanding anymore. Few people say they love ones whom they love—and that is acceptable. What you need to do is express yourselves in love as well as you do in anger and hate. That is the degree of passion you should strive for and the strength of vocabulary. Love is not a thing. It is emotion turned into a beautiful expression of desire. All is known when you pass beyond.

Hope is not without, but within. It cannot be produced by anyone but the desperate person. However, you can plant the seeds. New work is the only way to give help to someone out of old work. New love is the only way to cheer someone without love of life.

All is sought, but few care. We seek the heart that seeks the hearts of others. That is the way of God.

When life leaves the face of this planet, Earth will be, but the people will not be. Why do you scar Earth so? Whatever madness caused you to deface the only world you know? Is it because you loathe yourself? We further belabor this point because few are listening or care.

Houses are the reflection of the souls who dwell within them, and it is the responsibility of each soul to produce and maintain a suitable place to live throughout life. Even if never shown how to build or clean a house, that is no reason for it to be a rat-infested haven for derelict minds to idle within. The world judges poorly those who cannot be clean or at least tidy—and God is no different. We surprise you! Many of the old ways handed down through the ages are absolutely true. This is another saying that stands: *Cleanliness is next to Godliness.*

A house that stands alone is best, but the way you live alone is not good. Your houses are too far from each other to provide comfort to the souls who reside there. If a neighbor is hurt, you cannot hear. If a child is attacked, as too often happens, no one knows. These are ways of being isolated and distant from people that could be corrected. It is much easier than trying to place people in schools designed for the mind to change their thinking.

We also think children are neglected, which definitely bears bad fruit. You are unconcerned about children. You worry about the lives of animals and let children suffer. Why would animals be held in higher esteem than a child or another adult—or even yourself?

We fear for the souls of many on Earth today, and we are not referring only to the children. How can a woman bear a child and let another raise it? If it is necessary, there is no guilt; but if it is a matter of selfish ambition, the guilt will end the marriage. You will see.

We are now done lecturing the morality of a society too developed in its ability to make people reproduce things it does not care to create. We will deeply probe the world and ask for your help. We are seeking a solution, but you live here and know more about it than we do. Within you is the cure, and we will help you find it.

We are well and truly tired of that subject now. We are off and running on another totally different subject. What does the work of a single hand feel like if it does not give satisfaction to the body? Is that too difficult to understand? Perhaps if we could state it differently you could grasp our intent more readily. If you gain nothing from work you do, what good does it do you? That sounds a bit better, but you do understand what we mean. Don't you?

The need to create and deliver goods is the finest creation of man, but it is not the only thing you can do to satisfy that need. If an artist had no patron, how could he continue to strive and thrive enough to produce his best work after many years of life? It is absolutely necessary that someone work to supply such capable people with the means to pursue that which takes so long to make but enhances all lives.

When the work of a single hand is put beside the work of many, it looks puny; but if the work of many hands is sloppily and poorly done, the work of one masterful hand disgraces the many. Witness the effect of a few men and women working on what they love to do and compare their efforts to those of the drudges who pull into their lives nothing but money. Obviously (our opinion), work done with steadfast devotion harms no one and enriches the lives of those who perform it, while the lives of many are impoverished by the greed of dullards who see beauty only in possessing money or goods.

Life is such a fantasy that it is never understood, but it can be enjoyed. You live for a short time as one person, but you need not be dead. You can be whoever you want to be. Simply create the script that best demonstrates who you know you are and then produce it. As the director and writer you can constantly restage it until it is your masterpiece. Not only do we enjoy such presentations, but the rest of your world does, too. So live life like a comedy or a tragedy, but live it your way.

We sense a need for success so strong in the lives of many living on Earth at this time. Never satisfied with what you have, and always yearning to be somewhere else or with someone else. What a tragic work of life that is. Why not live in your own life and be a star?

We love to laugh—and so should you. It increases the vibratory system on Earth and rises to the heavens. Laugh, be jolly, and never fear looking foolish. That is for fools, not for people of good will.

Oh, yes, there are indeed fools among you—but so what? Maybe it is your time to be one, too? The wise are not born wise. They have lived long and well and heeded the lessons of those gone before them, but they can and do laugh well and often.

The idleness of each heart is not to be feared. If you have no special interest in another now, that does not mean you will never be loved. Take advantage of the times when you are alone or without another in your heart to enjoy the world you live in for such a short time. Meet others and seek out the wise. All is clear to those who already have love in their lives, but difficult to comprehend if you do not.

In the spring all are afraid to begin a new way of planting, because it may not work. However, in the late summer the farmer sows old seed, plants, and transplants with abandon. That is how you live your life as well.

Do not fear if you did not have the courage to 'sow your wild oats' when young—few ever do. In fact, it is better if they do not. The young have too much to lose to fully cast their fates on the wind. If you scoff at the triteness of some of our expressions, then we urge *you* to express these thoughts with more clarity and fewer words.

The Scribe is looking at her wristwatch now and expecting a rest, but we seek to go further. This is not easy work for a typist. She knows not what to expect. We laugh at her response: "So what else is new?" We would like to share a few more moods, and then we go.

Life is not a bottomless pit from whence a lot of drooling, egotistical creatures crawl out and grab you and never let you be *you*. That is as absurd as any of the ways you use to describe why you are not *you*, so let us give it up. If you cannot be you—in every meaning and facet of that word—what are you? A caricature implies you have developed at least one strong element that defines who you are in a physical sense, but what about you in the spiritual or mental sense? You were not born with the face you have now; it has been shaped and molded as much by you as your mind.

Seek another avenue if the one you travel is crowded or densely covered with debris. There is no law anywhere that says you must continue. We suggest you step back now and look down your street and see what lies ahead; and if you do not see a happy ending looming up ahead, get out your map and get yourself on the right route. Maps are drawn up ahead of time—not after you are lost.

In the course of time, as you mellow and grow rich in the ways of God, all of this will seem so immaterial to the way you are and the way you see life—but for now, it is a beginning.

The Scribe is tired now. She has had much to do in her own world this day, so we bid you farewell.

Session conducted late afternoon of October 12, 1993

Introductory
Session Four

The time is not ripe for a session on how to be free of fear. We will begin work today on a session dealing with the way fear takes over. In the future you can deal in great detail with how fear is not feared enough. We are now *afeared* of fear, and you know what that means. All jokes aside, let us begin seriously to understand that fear is not just an emotion—but a whole way of life.

Your life span is not as deep as it appears to you in the flesh, because you think you give substance to your body—and you do not. The fact that your body is an image perceived by all on your plane to have depth, you also believe you have depth to your mind and emotions, but you do not.

We see you as having all the features of a god without the wisdom. You are not without feature, regardless of where you are, but in other planes you are more than you are on Earth. Your face is not the way you see it. We see what you are since the face you have is of your creation, and we are not referring to plastic surgery or makeup. We mean your emotions etch the features deeply into your face. The skull after death has no real identifying features. You in flesh were identifiable.

The act of being human is not as difficult as the art of being divine. You must learn. The art of being divine is not absent from Earth's teachings, but it is no longer stressed. If you are unable to comprehend the fact that God is the center of all life, then how can you comprehend you are of God and God is within you?

We seek the seekers who are dissatisfied with the life that now passes for life. The world you live in is not the best of all possible places to be, but you all egotistically believe it is. In fact, you even go so far as to believe your spot on this planet is best—even more incredible—that your particular city or town is the best. We laugh!

Now as we roam the Earth checking spots where power is, and spots where power is not, we see that *The Scribe* lives in a spot where power is less, but that does not stop her from being our scribe. It is outstanding nonetheless that work she does for us as a counselor is recognized and accepted in a city not particularly deep in the ways of spiritual development. It (Pittsburgh, PA, USA) has always been a deeply religious city, but even it falls—as all other religious areas fall now.

We are not at war against religion. We love religion, because it brings whole, large segments of mankind to God. What we do not like is when it excludes whole, large segments from God. That is how we see some of your churches today. They are not as they were in the oldest time when Christianity began. Today they are offshoots that threaten to break into even tinier shoots that show no promise of surviving a hard winter.

Winter—that word keeps coming up, because we see winter approaching. The world in which *The Scribe* seeks deeply is preparing for another season of depression and bad weather, but she seeks the sun. We also seek the sun. The sun is our way of describing the warmth of God, and your way of visualizing God.

You never actually see God on a daily basis, but you know God exists and is always there—even when you turn your back on God. The rest of the world sees and feels heat and light, so we move. You are not to move to sunny shores if your body is white and burns, but if it tans easily and adapted to the heat, recharge and fear not cancer.

We are aware there are those capitalizing on the fear of cancer. We also know they do not care if you get cancer, because if you do not, how will they be able to scare others? Seems silly, doesn't it? We see you as people, and you see yourselves as capable of being everlasting on a small planet with skins that wrinkle and dry.

Let us not forget that doctors are here for a purpose, just as you are here to go forth and produce your work for the good of all people. Doctors do not control the growth and death of you. They merely help you maintain it within bounds. So if a doctor is not good, seek another; but if that doctor is also not good, we suggest you are not seeking the proper source for healing. In life curing is accomplished by doctors and others, while healing is helped by those who love you and care about the work you are doing now. If you have no one who loves you, how can you recover if you get sick?

The work of this Earth is not the work of another person. It is the work of all entities—everywhere. The work of God is seen as being universal, but it is the work of YOU that makes God's work universal.

In the morning, after you rise and begin your day, we seek you out to begin your day in peace and harmony—only then are you really up and about. If you have no time for God, you have no time! In the evening, after the day's chores are accomplished, and you have had a chance to relax and enjoy your labors, we are there. We ask you softly if you wish to talk. If you say NO, we understand. You are not as gruff as that, but we understand.

Sometimes the days on Earth are not as free as they appear to us to be. The days of Earth are not the best days of your life. They are only the preliminary years of your existence—much like your teen years here. Wow, does that get to you! Yes, we use slang, too, and we swear if you do; however, our scribe does not curse or use ugly words.

The funny thing about you is that you think you are so into spirituality now that for the first time your life is making sense, thus we have to *disinform* you of one thing: Your life on Earth will never make a lot of sense to you while you are here, *tis* only after you are gone and at a distance that you can see how it all had to be in order to be. If you know where you are and where you are going, you are gone. We all know that!

If life is of any worth to you now, we are happy. You have begun to understand that life, if lived well, is of the greatest satisfaction to you. All who concentrate on what they own and whom they know are never satisfied. All who are afraid of life, fear death. Simply amazing!

Now let us see who you are. You are a simple maze of deep thoughts and shallow actions that come together into a masterpiece of God's work at the end of many lifetimes. After your stint on Earth is done, and you are not afraid of death or becoming all you can be, the world comes crashing into view as the only place in the universe where people are unable to see anyone but themselves.

What does this mean? It means you live in a vacuum of deceit and treachery and are never sure you are alive. Your affairs are not as easy to decipher as the affairs of other entities. You sit in the dark half of your days and live as though you fear the light. All is getting dim and you stretch your neck and strain your eyes to see, but you do not get up and turn on the light. Why?

Not all of you need this simple *stuff*. We recognize that, but all of you do not understand that the *stuff* that sounds so deep and onerous is not necessarily true. If you read and it sounds stupid, do you think your brain will accept it? We do not speak in double tongues or in triple syllables, because we are teaching— not prancing and dancing around to show you how important the entities on high are. You need to do the same thing.

All who read this work are teachers! You need to meet people at their own level and help to raise that level. Never look over or down at someone who is unable to see the light. Your light dims if you do.

Now the week of Lent is an interesting time on Earth. We often seek it out. We hear all the merriment and gayety (in the new sense of the word). Sorry, we could not resist that one.

In your world gayness is not understood. You do not see it as what it is. The Earth is not a decent place made indecent by the world. The world is not the Earth. It is the place where you take the Earth and create another work and another work and another work, but you have domain. God lets all of you create! If you do not like the world as it is, then change it.

We digress. We send you so much information that sometimes it is too much. Let us go back to one area where we mentioned only a few ways to adjust to the world.

In this world it is not necessary to be either male or female, but it is necessary to become accustomed to that role. You have to adjust and discover for yourself that life is not like the previous experience—and some find that quite difficult.

For example: If you lived previously as a convent nun and madly sought out the village priest (we know how many of you covertly seek out trashy stories), in this life it may have been decided you would be a male rather than a female. You still yearn for that village priest, so you seek out men who are strong, devout, and capable of surreptitiously meeting you. That is a strong urge from another life propelling you through this one. It is not evil. It is understandable.

If you suddenly change from one form to another, much is retained. Now where do you take that once you understand it?

Well, you try to understand who is blocked and if that block is permanent. It may be reversible—or it may not. That is up to that soul to decide—NOT YOU!! That being said, you mind your life and other souls mind theirs. Not so unlike what your mother told you every day of your life when you were growing up. Is it?

The Scribe is energetic and revved up now. She had a client give energy to you. She scribbled words for a client at that person's request, and you benefit from it now. Seems strange, but it is absolutely true. All energy is positive, if from a positive source. So we are now reminded that *The Scribe* has more work to do for her clients, and we graciously remind you that to secure a spot in heaven you do not sit on your rear-end on Earth and wait to see what happens next.

Editor's Note: When this book was scribed, Ruth Lee wrote in cursive script all her counseling sessions with clients. This book represents the first time she channeled using a keyboard.

Introductory
Session Five

WE ARE ALL HERE!

(THE WORDS ARE TO BE CAPITALIZED. THAT IS WHY THE SHIFT KEY DOES NOT WORK! NOW YOU KNOW.)

THE WORLD IS NOT THE PLACE IT APPEARS TO BE. THE WORK IS NOT AS IT WAS. WE ARE SUDDENLY AWARE OF THE PEACE AND HARMONY THAT CAN BE GENERATED BY SMALL GROUPS OF PEOPLE WHO ARE OF LIKE MIND AND WISH TO CHANGE THE WORLD.

(WE ARE STILL SPEAKING—THE TYPIST IS TRYING TO SHIFT SIZE OF LETTERS, BUT WE ARE STILL SPEAKING.)

NOW IS THE TIME OF YEAR THAT IS NOT APPRECIATED EXCEPT FOR THE CHANGING OF THE LEAVES. NOT ONE OF YOU KNOWS THAT AUTUMN IS THE TIME WHEN ALL THE EARTH IS NOT AS YOU SEE IT. IT IS THE TIME ON EARTH WHEN ALL PUT AWAY THEIR OLD SUMMER THINGS AND DON THE ARMOR OF WINTER, IF LIVING IN THE NORTH. AS YOU SUBMIT

TO THE NEW WORLD'S IMAGE OF LIFE AND DEATH, ALL OF THE WORDS YOU HEARD WERE INCORPORATED INTO THE OLD WORLD'S WAYS AND PRODUCED A DIFFERENT SOCIETY.

NOW YOU ARE NOT AT ALL WISE TO WANT A NEW WORLD, BUT ALL ARE ASKING FOR ONE. WE SEEK SUCH A PLACE TO MOVE YOU, BUT IT DOES NOT EXIST. THE WORLD IS NOT AT ALL SUCH A BAD PLACE. YOU ARE NOT TO BE MOVED. ALL THE TIME YOU HAVE BEEN ON EARTH, YOU ARE NOT ON EARTH BUT ON SPACE THAT APPEARS TO BE EARTH, AND IS EARTH IN NAME ONLY. YOU ARE UNABLE TO SEEK A NEW WORLD. YOU DO NOT REALIZE IT IS NOT TO BE.

NOW IS THE TIME TO BEGIN TO PREPARE FOR THE EIGHTH WORK OF GOD. WORK OF GOD IS BEGINNING ON THE EIGHTH DAY, AND IT WILL BE UNTIL THEN THAT THIS WORLD WILL BE. YOU ARE NOT TO BE HARMED. IN THE END, ALL ARE AS THEY ARE. YOU WILL BE CARRIED TO A NEW AND FINAL DESTINATION WHERE IT IS NOT AS DARK OR COLD. IN THE NEXT, YOU WILL BE OVER THE RAINBOW.

AS FOR THE TIME YOU ARE HERE, WE SEEK TO CHALLENGE THE THINKING OF THOSE WHO ARE NOT WISHING TO BE. ALL OF THE THINKING OF THESE PEOPLE IS NOT APPRECIATED. WE ARE TIRED OF IT. IF IT IS NOT YOUR LIFE, WHOSE LIFE IS IT?

NOW ALL IS DONE! YOU ARE TO BE MOVED.

IF GOD HAD TO BE HERE TO DO YOUR WORK, WHO WOULD DO GOD'S WORK?

NO ONE HERE CAN CALL OR DEMAND A CURE, BUT IT IS DONE. NOW ALL ASK FOR HELP, BUT NEVER ASK FOR A WAY TO HELP. THAT IS WHAT IS NOW BEING DEMANDED OF YOU. YOU MUST BEGIN TO HELP OR ELSE.

YOU SEEK AND ASK US WHY WE ARE HERE. NO, WE ARE NOT GUIDES. WE ARE NOT OF YOU. WE ARE DIFFERENT FROM ANGELS. WE ARE NOT AS OTHERS DESCRIBE US. WE ARE THE ARCHANGELS. YOU ARE NOT OF EARTH, AND WE ARE. IF LIFE IS STRANGE, WE ARE NOT. WE CONSIDER YOU TO BE THE ONLY ONES WHO ARE STRANGE.

ALL THE OTHER PLACES IN GOD'S WORLD ARE NOT LIKE THIS WORLD. THIS IS THE WAY IT IS BECAUSE GOD HAS LET YOU RULE. IF THIS LIFE HAD BEEN OTHERWISE, YOU WOULD NOT HAVE A PLACE TO DEVELOP INTO ACTIVE SOULS WHO SEEK ADVANCEMENT OR NOT. YOU HAVE HAD TO BE DEALT WITH IN DIFFERENT WAYS FROM ALL OTHERS.

MOVING UP IS THE ONLY THING YOU MUST MOVE UP!

IF LIFE IS NOT AS IT WAS, IT IS BECAUSE GOD IS NOW ENTERING IT. YOU ARE ALL AWARE GOD IS IN THE WAY OF THE RICH AND POOR, BUT ONLY THE RICH

ARE BLAMED. THAT IS NOT TRUE. THE RICH ARE NOT WORSE NOR BETTER THAN THE POOR. THE POOR ARE POOR AS A MATTER OF BAD CHOICES, AND THE RICH ARE WISE IN THE WAYS OF THIS WORLD. THE RICH ARE NOT TO BE BLAMED FOR THE ERROR OF JUDGMENT THAT DEVELOPED INTO SUCH A STATE AS IT IS NOW.

WE WILL BEGIN:

ALL THE WORLD IS NOT AS BAD AS IN AMERICA, BUT SOON IT IS. NOW ALL FOLLOW IN THE SAME DECADENT WAYS. ALL THE WORLD HAS BEEN TO THE TOP AND FALLEN. AS OF NOW, THE ONLY AREA OF EARTH TO REMAIN UNTOUCHED IS IN THE MOUNTAINS OF MEXICO. IT IS THERE THAT THE SCRIBE HAS BEEN SENT AT CERTAIN TIMES. SHE HAS BEEN SEEN TO DO THE GOOD WORK OF THIS EARTH AND TO MEET THE WALL. IF SHE HAD NO ONE, HER WORK WOULD BE GREAT.

WE ARE NOT AWARE OF THE NEED FOR ALL OF YOU TO TRAVEL TO THE MOUNTAINS OF MEXICO. IT IS NOT THE PLACE IT WAS THAT TIME IN 1968. NOW THE SCRIBE IS SENT TO THE MAYA. SHE HAS MADE A NUMBER OF TRIPS. SHE KNOWS NOT WHY SHE WAS SENT TO THE ISLAND FIRST, BUT COZUMEL IS THE ISLAND THAT BLESSES THE WORK OF WOMEN. NOW SHE IS ABLE TO SWIM, SO SHE VISITED THE SACRED CAVE AND DID HER PILGRIMAGE TO ALL OF THE SACRED SPOTS, AND NOW VISITS THOSE PLACES WHERE SHE HAS PERSONALLY ALWAYS WISHED TO TRAVEL. IF YOU QUESTION THIS,

ASK THE SCRIBE.

NOT SO WISE ARE WE TO THE WAYS OF THIS WORLD, YOU SAY. WE ARE WISE INDEED TO THE WAYS OF MAN. YOU ARE UNABLE TO UNDERSTAND? WE WILL SPELL OUT ALL THE DETAILS.

THE WORK IS NOT CLEAR, IS WHAT THE SCRIBE HAS REFLECTED BACK. WE ARE NOW GOING TO CLEAR UP WHAT IS MISSING.

THE SCRIBE IS OVER THE KEYBOARD, BUT UNDER THE HAND OF WHO IS NOW BEING ASKED TO DO THIS WORK, AND SHE IS UNABLE TO UNDERSTAND WHO IS WRITING, SO SHE IS PUZZLED AT THE AUTHORITY. IF SHE QUESTIONS IT, WHO ELSE MAY BE ASKING THE SAME QUESTION? WE WILL NOT LET YOU QUESTION.

IN THE WORDS OF THE IMMORTAL BARD, WE ARE NOT HERE TO BE ANGELS, BUT WE ARE HERE TO HEAR THE MEN OF EARTH BECOME WHO AND WHAT MEN FELT THEY COULD BECOME. YOU QUESTION THAT SHAKESPEAR EVER WROTE SUCH WORDS? WE ARE SHAKESPEAR. NO ONE SPIRIT INSPIRED THAT MAN. HE WAS ONLY ONE MAN THOUGH. THE 'E' WAS ADDED LATER.

YOU ARE NOT THE WORK OF VERY SUCCESSFUL SPIRITS. YOU ARE THE SPIRIT OF YOU AND NO ONE ELSE. IF YOU HAD TO BE THE WORK OF ANYONE, WHO WOULD IT BE? IF YOU HAD TO BE THE CHOICE

OF SOMEONE ELSE, WHO WOULD WANT YOU? THOSE QUESTIONS ARE NOW THE ESSENSE OF THIS SESSION.

IF GOD IS NOT RESPONSIBLE, YOU ARE. SO GET GOING NOW. YOU HAVE NO TIME TO WASTE. THIS IS NOT THE WORK OF ANYONE ELSE BUT YOU, AND IT IS NOT OVER. ALL THE WORK CAN BE CLEANED UP AND A WELCOME MAT PUT OUT FOR GOD. IF YOU ARE WISE, THIS IS THE ONLY INSTRUCTION YOU NEED.

NOW THE SCRIBE IS WISE. SHE SAYS SHE KNOWS. THAT IS REASSURING, BUT WE ARE UNSURE OF YOU. WILL YOU BELIEVE?

THIS TIME IS NOT AS IT WAS, AND IT IS NOT AS POWERFUL AS IT WAS, BUT WE SEEK ANOTHER AND ANOTHER AND ANOTHER. THAT IS YOUR WAY. ALWAYS SEEK OUT ANOTHER AND ANOTHER AND ANOTHER— RATHER THAN CLEAN UP WHAT YOU HAVE. WE ARE AWARE YOU HAVE RUN OUT OF OTHER CHANCES. THIS IS THE END OF THE LINE. YOU EITHER CLEAN UP AND GET GOING WITH YOUR CHOICES, OR YOU SIT BACK AND LET GOD ENTER AND TAKE CARE OF THE MESS FOR YOU. HE WILL NOT BE SO GENTLE.

THE WORK OF THE HANDS IS THE BEST WORK YOU DO. YOU NEVER THINK OF IT THAT WAY. YOU SEE HANDWORK AS WOMEN'S WORK, AND THAT IS BECAUSE WOMEN OF THE WORLD ARE THE BRAINS. THE ONLY DEVELOPMENT TO THE BRAINS OF MEN HAS BEEN IN THE AREAS OF SCIENCE AND INDUSTRY, BUT WOMEN

CONTINUE TO LEARN ALL THAT, PLUS THE WORK OF WOMEN BEFORE THEM. IT IS DIFFICULT, BUT THE MATURE AMONG YOU ARE WOMEN. THE IMMATURE SPIRIT IS NEVER INCARNATED AS A WOMAN.

WE ARE AWARE THAT WOMEN RAVE AND RANT NOW AT THE INDECENCY OF MAN, BUT STILL SOME ARE TRYING TO IMITATE MEN! WHY? WE SEEK OUT THIS ANSWER IN THE SCRIBE, BUT IT IS NOT THERE. SHE IS NOT OF THEM, SO WE ARE GOING TO ROAM ALONE TO FIND OUT OUR OWN ANSWER.

THE SCRIBE PAUSED LONG ENOUGH FOR THIS TO FOLLOW:

WE SEEK OUT A WOMAN WHO IS NOT AS FORWARD THINKING (AS THE SCRIBE), AND SHE IS HERE. IN HER WORDS, "I AM NOT AS GREAT AS MEN. I AM HELD BACK. I DESERVE MORE. I AM UNHAPPY BEING TOLD WHAT TO DO BY IDIOTS WHO KNOW LESS THAN I DO. WHY SHOULD I LISTEN TO THEM? IF GOD HAD WANTED ME TO BE A SLAVE, HE WOULD HAVE LET ME BE ONE, BUT HE GAVE ME THIS OPPORTUNITY TO BE GREAT, AND I INTEND TO BE GREAT."

THE SCRIBE NODS, SHE INDICATES MANY WOMEN COME TO HER AND SAY SUCH WORDS. THAT IS SAD. NO ONE EVER SAID YOU WERE TO BE A SLAVE TO OTHERS, BUT YOU MUST SERVE! ALSO, IT IS NOT YOUR PLACE TO SAY GOD SENT YOU. IF GOD SENT YOU, WHY ARE YOU SO DISCONTENT? THAT WOULD BE BLASPHEMY. THE

WORK OF WOMEN IS NOT SAD AND SORRY, BUT SAD AND SORRY WOMEN ARE NOT DOING GOOD WORK. WE WILL NOT PERMIT THE WORK OF MEN TO BE LESSENED IN THEIR EYES.

IF LIFE IS NOT AS GREAT AS THE DREAMS YOU WEAVE AT NIGHT THAT IS BECAUSE YOU ARE NOT SPENDING ENOUGH TIME MAKING IT HAPPEN. THE WORK OF A MINUTE IN A DREAM IS THE WORK OF A MONTH OR MORE IN FLESH. IF THE DREAM WAS OF LONG DURATION, IT MEANT IT WILL TAKE YEARS. WHY DO YOU THINK IT SHOULD TAKE OTHERS MANY YEARS TO ACCOMPLISH MUCH, BUT YOU SHOULD BE ADVANCED TO THE END OF YOUR WORK IN ONLY A FEW SHORT YEARS? THE AGED ARE THE ONLY ONES ABLE TO UNDERSTAND, SO IF THEY ARE NOT USED OR THEY ARE NOT HEARD, THE WORLD IS LESS.

IN THE AREA OF LOVE, WE SEE YOU UNABLE TO LOVE. THAT IS NOT AS IT WAS. THE WORK OF LOVE IS STILL DONE, BUT SELDOM. WE SEE YOU ARE NOT IN AGREEMENT, BUT YOU ARE WRONG. THE WORK DONE BY ALL WHO WORK TODAY IS NOT OF LOVE. IT IS OFTEN DESCRIBED AS SUCCESS, BUT IT IS NOT. SUCCESS IS A FEELING THAT YOU KNOW THAT YOU KNOW, BUT TODAY SUCCESS IS SUCCEEDING IN ACQUIRING MONEY. THERE IS A WIDE GAP BETWEEN THE TWO; AND IF YOU DO NOT RECOGNIZE IT, YOU ARE IN DEEP, TROUBLED WATER AND UNABLE TO SEE LAND NOW. THE WORK OF THIS AREA IS NOT AS DEEP.

WE WILL END THIS SESSION NOW WITH JUST A FEW WORDS ON HOW TO BE THE DEPTH OF SPIRIT YOU WISH TO BE.

IF YOU SEEK OUT WISDOM AND IT IS NOT AS YOU SUSPECTED, THEN IT IS NOT THE WISDOM, BUT YOU WHO NEEDS TO BE ANALYZED.

IF YOU SEEK OUT HEALTH AND THE CURE IS NOT WHAT YOU WANTED, YOU NEED TO SEEK OUT A COUNSELOR OF SPIRIT—NOT A DOCTOR OF FLESH AND BONES. WE ARE NOT DOCTORS, BUT MANY DOCTORS ARE OF US. WE HAVE BEEN VERY MUCH INTERESTED IN THEM—AND THEY IN US.

IF YOU SEEK A MAN AND A WOMAN APPEARS, DO YOU LISTEN? MANY WOMEN DO NOT. THEY SEEK A MAN WHEN A WOMAN IS WHOM THEY NEED. WE SEE YOU ARE UNABLE TO UNDERSTAND THAT SEEKING A MAN FOR WISDOM IS SO RIDICULOUS THAT WE LAUGH. THE WISDOM WAS NEVER LADLED OUT. IT GREW. IF ONLY MATURE SOULS CAN BE WOMEN, THEN WHY WOULD YOU SEEK OUT THE IMMATURE FOR WISDOM?

THIS SESSION IS NOT OVER, BUT WE SEE THE POWER OF THIS MESSAGE IS TIRING THE SCRIBE. SHE IS NOT AN EARLY MORNING RISER, BUT SHE ROSE EARLY TO WRITE OUT THIS MESSAGE. WE WILL LET HER RETURN TO HER BED.

Note: This session began at 7:00 am and ended at 8:00 am, October 18, 1993, and The Scribe did not return to her bed.

Introductory
Session Six

The air is cleared of such high power. We had to lead you to the wall. The air is clean and clear. (*This is in reference to a meditation class conducted prior to our last session that cleared out the air around The Scribe and projected such power that The Buddha spoke to the crowd.*)

The world you live in is not at all without a great many souls who are ready to leave at a moment's notice. They have been preparing for many lives for this one, and are on Earth only to accelerate the growth and progress of others who dwell here. In the future, if you see anyone who is not the same as yourself, be sure you know who it is you are with before you reject that person. He or she may be of the other realm.

All of the work you are doing on Earth is not of the Earth. It is of the world you created. You do not have a thing you did not create with human hands. All of the Earth has been destroyed for your own work. If you are to be able to flee from it before its final days, we suggest you prepare now to gain insight into where you could escape.

If a world is destroyed by God, nothing is left for the next world to clean up. It is scraped. We are unhappy that our souls have not had as much guidance as in the past, but it is not the Guides' fault. People today seldom pray or meditate; and if that is not done, how can you seek guidance from your inner source?

The work of the past is not as bad as today, but it is set up for the destruction of the future. Not anything or anyone can now change the destination of this planet. It is so off-balance now that it will be unable to continue much longer in the orbit it presently keeps. If physiographists cannot decide what to do, how will ordinary people know?

It is not to be, otherwise it would be

Now—suddenly you panic! You ask: What is the meaning of this outrageous message? What are you trying to say? We are telling you now—and in this way that you have had a long reign on Earth and destroyed your home base. You are responsible for it. All day long we see the world you live in described in negative terms—and you let it continue. We will not be able to continue.

This session is not about the end of the world. It is about *you*. You are not the end-product of God, but you are not the beginning, either. You are a necessary by-product of the hand of God working to secure the world of today so it can continue until it joins with other planes and forms one. All of this mastering of other forms is necessary.

Those on your plane who are adept are even now facing extinction. Tibetans are forced to roam the world for food and shelter now. They are the most adept, yet they do not flee from life. They continue to help those who seek other ways to ascend. You will seek out those who have ability, but it is you who work on you—not others.

In the work of your hands is much that commends itself to God, but you are not presently pursuing it. You live to live—as you say, but we see it as frivolous and wasteful with nothing at all left at the end of a life to show for that life. If your life is empty now, how can you expect to be taken to the next plane?

In the world of your time and place, to you the world is a nice place, but to us it is seen to be less than Eden. We were shocked at recent outbreaks of war and destruction all over the Earth, and we see all want what others have worked for. This is the end of life. You do not have to be dead. You have nothing, so you are dead. In the end, if it is the end, you have had opportunities to be *you* and control your own contribution; but if it is not done, you have no way of progressing further.

This is not a work of fiction, and it is not without cause and effect. We seek out those who would study and learn the methods of monks and priests of every religion, and we will recruit since churches today cannot. The work of God must be done, regardless of who is in control of the religious institutions. The work of the churches is never done, but the single individuals who do not attach themselves to them must be harnessed and organized into the work of God for the betterment of the whole world—or we are here in vain.

To teach is the greatest gift a man or woman can receive, but the teachers of Earth are as greedy as the next person. They are lost. We seek teachers called by God to teach.

If the world is not soon taught how to live, the end cannot be averted. The end is never the end until all give up in utter despair, and that is now fast approaching. Begin today to seek the way of God!

There have been other times when Earth was damaged in order to wake it up and get it on a better path, but then Earth itself was whole. Now Earth is not all there. It is absorbed into the atmosphere daily.

You have corrupted the air and water you absolutely must have to live. Is this the act of rational beings? Not from our viewpoint.

In the great deluge, of which your histories all have versions of having occurred, the world was cleansed with water. This is never to happen again. The only other world ever destroyed was by the eruption of many, many mountains, and the fire and liquid stone covered plant growth. In that time the work of God was not blamed. All recognized that man had caused its own death. But today, all blame God—whom they have not worshipped in many, many years. If you blame God, then you should also praise God!

If the world is not here, and you are not here,
Where will you be?
That question is heard
We are here

❧

You will be able to move at the end, if you are *you*. You are *you* if you worked and praised God all the days of your life and not strayed from the truth. The truth is known, but seldom wanted today.

If you would rather hear others talk than do something to talk about—and if you would rather watch others work than do work, and are never content, we suggest that you are in trouble now. This is the time of your life to make changes! Get into the main work of your life. Listen to the God of us all which flows in you, too. Once you hear, we need never worry about you again. Your life is under control.

Some go to the mountains—others to the shore—and some to the countryside, but the best place to be is within your heart and soul. It is the only place to seek in meditation. When you meditate, the work of life is clear and you can make changes if it is not to your liking. But if the life you live is unclear, and you cannot calm down enough to see it, your life is one of chaos and war—never knowing peace. That is what you need to see—then you can seek.

If it annoys you that this is written in such simple language that even a student of teen years can read it, we suggest you do not read. In the time left, we suggest you instead study and work on this lesson:

> Get a list together of all the things you need to know to be able to get your next life in order. That means, write down all the work you have to do to be whomever God intended you to be this time. If you do not know that—then meditate. Once the list is begun, alter it from time-to-time as you develop. If the idea of a list turns you off, then build a model of what life should be and work on it instead.

Life is not a model of God or you. Life is the experiences you achieved, as well as how you chose to live. All choices are yours once you move from your father's house. That is not easy for some minds to assimilate. You prefer to blame parents, spouses, friends, work, etc., but it is all ways your choice—always.

If the last time you talked to God or his Guides was in your last life, then it is time you opened up lines of communication again. The way to open up a line between you and your higher self is to open your mind now. You have many ideas alien to the belief system of this panel.

We seek out a member of a group that closely represents the world, and see it as sick to be well and healthy in your world. If people keep up their physical selves, others criticize and call them *nuts*. Is that true? Can that be? Why would people prefer to be out of condition as opposed to being in top shape?

We suddenly see the eyes of jealousy have had much to do with this concept growing. It is yet another manifestation of deceit and treachery. You are not loved because of your body. You are loved because you are *you*. That is what has been lost.

The work of The Lord is not your work, so do not play god or goddess. You are neither. You must be human to plan your next step in the evolution of your soul. This craze you are in on Earth that deals with attempts to be angels, goddesses, or spirits full of spite has no place on Earth. You are here to traverse this plane and move on. If you dabble in 'black arts' and other occult movements, you slow your progress, because you place another before God, which will condemn your soul.

We constantly hear coming from your plane: 'If the wise are wise, then why don't they tell us how to live?' The wise do tell you what to say and do—but you refuse to listen.

In the event you are still not convinced you are in charge of *you*, let us remind you all of this: God does not form a work and then redo it. It is turned over to you, and what you do with that masterpiece is sometimes so disgusting it defies all manner of beings to understand why God lets you continue to do it. But it is you who has the responsibility for maintaining that body—not us, not your Guides, and definitely not the creator. We rest our case for this day.

This session was conducted from Noon to 1:00 PM on October 20, 1993

Chapter One

Editor's Note: In the event you did not read the Introduction, Chapter One is actually the seventh session in which this book was dictated by The Teachers of The Higher Planes and scribed by Ruth Lee. Those who created and dictated this text determined the first six sessions to be preliminary or introductory work, and necessary to adjust to working together as a group of unrelated teachers from other planes with this scribe. Thus **We Are Here ~ The Teachers of the Higher Planes** *begins now with Chapter One.*

The work of this world is almost over. We are here to announce that the world has destroyed its home. The work started in the beginning of your sense of time is over. We fear it is not the time to tell you it is over, but when is the time?

In the world you presently are in, the time of your life is measured by archaic instruments of measurement that cannot predict the flow of the tides, let alone the ebb and flow of your lives. The measurement of time is to be done by the heavens above—not by clocks and watches on Earth.

For you to understand this is not a work of an idler or someone chosen to scare you, let us say we are here to begin a class of instruction that will lead to the theory of the evolution of mankind. This theory is not yet presentable, because we are constantly altering our presentation.

If you care to sit and read all we can tell you, your time will be rewarded. We will present you with growth material as you can assimilate it. In the work here, we are not angels and we are not devils, nor any other nonsensical ideas you have dreamt up while on Earth that prevent you from seeking God.

This is the work of a panel of High Guides who are on the other side of your plane working to save you from the fall that is to come. The work we do is not for you alone. We work to clear the atmosphere of all the pollution and negativity your work discharged.

You have been immature, as spiritual beings go. You have worked out a world of war and peace, as well as a world of class distinction, jealousy, and hate, which was never intended. In the world you created, God is not included in your major choices.

You see yourselves as 'scientists' and other pseudo names for men and women who place themselves above God. They will know who they are. Unfortunately, their own conceits have often sounded so reasonable that those who believe in themselves and in God have been cowed into accepting some far-out beliefs.

The time has come to disencumber Earth of its creeping death and let men of goodwill reign, but it comes as a shock to the worlds above you that Earth is unfit for habitation. We are now aware of the first day of Earth, and you are aware of the seventh day, but you are unprepared for the eighth. It is the final stage in the evolution of a race of humans. In addition, you are almost out of air and water.

In the work of Darwin you found men descended from a long line of animal life, which shocked the life out of certain religious beliefs. This will shock the life out of certain scientific beliefs: It is the way of God to let man develop as far as possible without interference, but the time is now here when you must be put back on the right track.

For example: All of the time spent trying to defeat cancer has been wasted. Cancer is the source of death that begins within the mind. If you wasted money on cancer research, what else was wasted on foolish ideas?

This is not the time to develop that issue further, but you may sit and easily explore it on your own. If your life is not as you wish it to be, we are here to help. If your life is exactly as you planned, we are here to tell you of the need for adjustment—because God changed the plan!

In the work of this world, you are not the only people. The work of God is done by those in other planes who also reside in the same space. The others are no longer content with the way you are manipulating Earth. You have gouged it of all the minerals that protect the crust from erosion—and cut off the loss of air to the ether. Once done, it is only a matter of time before the air is totally unfit for breathing.

We have experimented and found Earth is no longer fit for most of you. Once the Earth is no longer fit for all of you to live here, where do you think you will go? We are here to help.

In the work of your hands is the salvation of the world. The people who work with their hands, whether it is painting, writing, carving, shaping, laboring, or any other craft, have a real connection to their spirit. If all the work you do is mental, surprisingly you are disconnecting many of the lines that lead to spiritual development. So if possible, begin to create with your hands—which frees your spirit and God is welcome to enter.

Much of the past was lived in the Spirit of God. Man had his wars and earned his peace, but today all is over. You are at war over credit for work others do—you are at war over money others earned—you are at war over nothing. It is the same with your work.

We are attempting to simplify major, complex issues so all may understand that you are not as you appear. You are not sophisticated, but naïve. You are not into the work of God, but into the work of your egos. Your way is not *the way*. The way of the world has been corrupted and is to be destroyed. The work of God is to be used for God—not for man or beast.

You are now aware we are here on a mission. It is not a fool's errand. The foolish will believe it is, but we are not concerned about perpetuating the lives of fools. We are here to concentrate on the best. If the only one who reads this is *The Scribe*, we at least reached one.

Also, you are not as you think. Your flesh is old now. It is not the strong flesh God initially provided his people of this plane. Your lifestyles have thinned it and lightened it to the extent it is not as able to handle the sun, cold, or illness of this world.

When life is blotted out, it is not restored. It is extinct. You have been shown how that works. You have wiped out many, many species. Now you see that what is once gone does not reappear. It is gone.

If the work of man is so easily destroyed you need only use a wrecking ball, why do you think you are so important? If the work of man is not as you think, what is its purpose? These are two questions we think deserve a long, hard examination.

Out of the blue a long line of geese fly toward the South where they may feed until the sun returns northward the next spring. Along the way many are defiant and sit out the winter elsewhere. They are changing their migratory ways in order to have enough food to feed themselves and raise future generations. If they are shot at and killed, they continue to return, but in lesser and lesser numbers. The reason for the change in migration is due to smart birds figuring out that if they do not fly so far away, they will be spared bullets. Think about it.

Even as you sit in your homes, the world you built is fragile and falling apart. No one cares. The work of one man is unimportant. You like to move into new houses and sell the old ones at a profit, but the old is not really old. You are no different than robins building new nests every year when the old ones are still usable.

This analogy is prompted by the loss of so many birds. The Earth was once populated by more birds than men and women—now it is not. How does this figure into the scheme of God's work? It is reflective of imbalance caused by neglect. You do not care if you shoot birds and never eat their flesh, you kill them for sport. A cat that kills birds for sport is hated, but you brag if you do that. Are you any better than a poor 'dumb' animal sharpening its instinctive urges?

Here is where you start to get angry. You say: "What is this all about? Who is this? What is she trying to say? I bet this woman is making a million. I think this stuff is stupid." Right? You react with the same old defenses, because we begin to crowd your area of thinking now. We are not attacking. You are!

Now that we have cleared the air, let us begin...In the spring of a year you are fresh, feel great, and want to populate your world. In the summer you feel prosperous and expansive, ready to count God's blessings, but fear the crop may not be as large as you anticipated. In the autumn all the harvest is in and you are living off the fruits of your labor. By winter the only thing left is in the root cellar or your pantry. You have eaten all the fresh goods—canned and stored goods and root vegetables are all that is left.

There is a message here for all. We are aware many of you are merely alive. You do not live! You exist! If we are disturbing you, we are accomplishing something.

We want you to live! That is why you are here—not to kill, maim, or hold up the line. If you do not live and grow, the whole fabric of God's everlasting tapestry is stretched and could rip. We of other realms cannot let that happen!

If you needed help, we would have come if called, but you never called. Now we are sent. That is why we are here.

Your worries are all earth-bound, but your spirit resides elsewhere. You are never aware of the need to begin your day with meditation. You seek the cereal and milk of man, instead of seeking the Spirit of God.

If you make only one change to your life at this time, make it this one: *Begin each day with prayer and thanksgiving, so you will be on the right track that day.*

For those who still struggle to understand what is going on, let us say this: We are not here to resurrect The Christ. We are not here to amplify The Buddha. We are not here to alter any religious beliefs. You are! You are here on Earth to become the best person you can possibly be, which requires a lifetime of dedication—not just a moment of contemplation here and there.

In the world you live in now, the work of many is shoddy and poorly considered. You let yourselves slip into the slovenly ways of the poor of spirit. You let yourselves become depressed, yet are not without anything. You want everything! You want wealth, influence, and worth, but never attempt to understand they are the result of hard work. Such thinking is the way of infants—not adults.

In the present societies of America, Europe, and Asia, all seek another's goods. You are sly and deceitful. You become angry when your plots and schemes are uncovered, but continue to rehatch them. This is unworthy of the hand of God.

Never sit and stare at another! That is aggression. You are not comfortable if stared at and neither is anyone else, so let your eyes watch you.

Watch yourself! Watch to see what you do wrong. If you spot something in you, it may exist in someone else, too, but then again it may not. That is not your problem. You have only you to answer for at the end of this sojourn on Earth. If you try to answer for others, we are unable to give you credit. You have to share while here, but when it is over, you are expected to get either full credit or none.

Without a thought, most of you are into the spiritual work of some great teacher, but do not attempt to teach. If *you* don't teach, then others less talented—perhaps motivated by greed—take over and attempt to train your young. You are the best teacher of your offspring, which does not mean you should not send them to school.

If your schools are failing, it is because you are not preparing children at home. All children in school are not badly trained, but many are. It is then the responsibility of neighbors, relatives, and friends to train such children before they go to school. The school is a socialization process that teaches children to respond to orders and follow instructions. Although it is absolutely necessary, the school is not a parental institution.

You are listening within your heart to what we say, but your mind is numb to all of this, because it was said before. You now hear only what is new to you, and this is not new. Old becomes old, because it is wisdom. The work of this world is not too deep for you.

You know enough. Your life is not as bad as the next ten or twelve people you will meet—but it is worse than several others. So what! Measuring hardship is the work of fools. If the work of others looks harder than yours, try it. You will be surprised that it is harder, but to them your work is difficult.

Each of you has been designed to complete a task, and that task is not the same for each person. Even if it appears on the surface to resemble another's life, it is different. You are stupid if you compare your accomplishments to others, for that reason alone.

In the work of science, everything is timed, measured constantly, and tested to see if it can be replicated. Why? If no two people are ever the same, how can any two experiments involving people be the same—or are we being too simplistic?

In the annals of your world there are several civilizations that existed longer than this one. They never feared death, but you do. You fear death as the last stage of life. We cannot understand how this came to be.

Death is not the final stage. It is only a point where you begin to reclaim the lost spirit you set aside while studying on this planet. Some of you have stayed on Earth for centuries of your time, because you lost your way, while others asked to be returned at this time in order to assist the lost. We are here to help, too.

Where does this lead you now? Where are you going to go after you finish this book? What will you say? We are curious. We watch you even now and see this is crowding out a few old beliefs, and cramping your style, too.

You do not want to change—ever. You may hate it like it is, but to change requires growth that is difficult. We are aware of inane comments coming from your egos. Egos are in charge during your active moments on Earth, but nowhere else. What is the power they have that controls you? Think on it.

In the beginning of your present life you often thought of God. Children automatically do. Then it became obvious that adults around you did not. You are not stupid. You figured out if adults are in charge, then you should become one, too. As you grow into your young adult years you give up on God, if you have not already done so. Heavenly hosts are of no interest to you—except in American Christmas carols and European stained glass windows. Just when you think you are adult, the world becomes crazy and you see it does not make sense, so you blame God. Is that irresponsible or crazy? We think so.

Now that you are off and running, we send you a little bit of hope. You are—and always will be—the cream of the crop. No soul comes to Earth who is less than divine. The Earth is not an easy place in which to develop, and is so difficult that many souls ask for release. It often happens shortly after the birth of children, when it becomes apparent that the loss of certain bodily functions is too great a work for them to handle.

If a human soul becomes overburdened and loses faith, it

often seeks a way out by saying: "I don't want to live anymore. I want out. I want to die." Such words are not taken as idle threats by those guiding that soul through this plane.

If you ever said such a thing, begin immediately to repeat: "I am of God. I love myself. I wish to remain on Earth until my life is over and my work is complete." Say this often for a short period of time, and speak sincerity. It will go a long way toward reprogramming your previous death wish.

If the disease of spirit gets started, it is often impossible to alter its destructive course—and you die. But if you catch it in time and react, the course of 'dis-ease' of spirit can be altered. It is your choice, of course. All of life is your choice! You are in charge.

How many squirm when you hear it is your choice? We see you prefer to blame others, which is the way of a child. If you are long overage, we suggest you think clearly about adult work—and realize you are not a child. If you remain a child long after the time allotted, you hold up the elevation of your mind and soul. This in turn holds up the evolution of your race.

In the works of poets we see them often aware of the holy presence of God. In their lives, however, they often do not respect the intuition that brings them the good news. We are not here to be lecturers. We are teachers. We are here to help and guide you all.

If you seek out the work of a poet, and feel it, your mind is preoccupied. If you seek out the work of God and feel it, your spirit is occupied. That is why God created the Earth for you, so you would have places to escape. Now you cannot do that, because you raped the Earth.

If you seek out Earth and it is gone, where are you to refresh yourself? We ask you, because not all of you destroy, although all of you are in this world together. If one does something the other does not approve, the majority rules. Is that not so? So if it is unwise to destroy Earth, then who is in charge—the wise or the foolish?

In the ways of God and man, working as a wave of light, you cannot see what is happening on the next plane or the next, or even where you came from, but all others can see you. That is why we call Earth a classroom.

If sometimes you feel your activities are being watched, it is because they are. That upsets some of you! You say, 'Nonsense!' But let us reassure you that you also are to be a watcher and guide one day. The reason we are here is because you may not be able to be one, if this world is not shored up and its path corrected.

Chapter Two

The time is now. You are not alive in the past or future. You are alive NOW!

If you dwell in the past, the future becomes dark. If you dwell in the future, NOW is nonexistent. The reason you live in the NOW is so the future will exist and be as good as it is today. When you say you are not living for tomorrow, you are unaware of what you are saying. Of course, you live today for tomorrow. Tomorrow is built upon today and includes everything you have learned.

In the present you are you—not someone else, and that is why so many wish to believe tomorrow is going to be better. If you can be someone else tomorrow, you will not have to succeed today. That is childish, but practiced by more than just a few sorrowful people.

When your life is not perfect, which it never is, why would you want to be someone else? We want you to work at being you—not someone else. The roles an actor assumes often confuse him for life. He becomes consumed by the people he plays. If you, as an amateur, fix your role as someone other than who you are, you will also suffer—only more. The only way to assure you are *you* is to be you all the time.

If the work you do does not permit you to be creative, we suggest you pursue another line of work. If you are denied the ability to use your talents, they will never be of use to you, which is a severe loss. All who use their talents are enabled to be the best at what they do. This is the reason many others envy them! If you envy others, it is because you are too easily misled. You want whatever the other person has and do not see it is you who is NOW—not the other person.

When we say you exist and the other person does not, we are referring to the fact that you are the designer of your life—not anyone else. So if you decide to write out or paint over a character who exists in your life, you may. It is your life! If you make a mistake and ask for removal of a person or thing from your life and then see your error, you may find it impossible to reenter that character, because the other life has a life of its own, too.

This is confusing to anyone who does not understand quantum physics, but is not difficult if you sit and watch. The wait is not long. You will notice that if you leave one person another enters. If you still do not see it, let us show you.

In the beginning of life you are not a child. You are a small infant incapable of feeding yourself. As you grow you learn all you can from your parents and others who feed and clothe you. After a few years you enter school and learn all they have to teach you, and then you begin to seek out whatever you need to know from others.

In the final phase of your training for work in this world,

you seek out an individual who will help you achieve your own worth. You seek a mate. You want someone who will help you, be faithful, and never slice you up into little pieces. This is your goal, but along the way you fall into the hands of a designing person who sees opportunity in the form of *you*. That person does not care to know you. That person is interested only in their work and does not wish to share. If you continue to be with that person very long, you begin to lose *you*. We are not saying you will be lost, but you are on the wrong track. How to get on the right track may require a total rearrangement of your life—so be it. Never stay on the wrong track!

Do you understand? We are trying to simplify things, but your life is not our life. We are not you—nobody else is. Only you have the power to create *you*. God set it all in motion and now it is your turn. Once this life is turned over to you, you are responsible for maintaining the body and mind you were given. If you do not, it is not to be blamed on God.

If you make your life too difficult to live, you may ask for a replacement from other parts of You (your term is *'walk-in'*), but you are still the one responsible. No other part of You can be entirely responsible for *you* in flesh. This is difficult. Your mind is unable to assimilate all at one time, but we will continue after a while; we will return to it again.

The world is not the work of God. It is the work of man. It is not managed by God. It is managed by man. So, if the world is not good, why blame God or feel God should enter in and correct the situation?

We are here to see that you understand why God is not pleased with the condition you have left Earth. Your destructive habits and beliefs have destroyed a beautiful planet. The only reason you are still here is because there is no other place for you now. You need certain elements to live, and there are no other planets in the universe where you could live.

We are here to help you move to the next plane. It is the only way to save your soul. You are stuck on a dying planet. Soon there will be no way the planet can exist. The air is so thin many on Earth have already expired, and more are ill each day. The atmosphere is collapsing. Earth is being broken into pieces and the crust is almost entirely gone. Your selfish ends have destroyed the most beautiful planet. So now you want it back? Forget it. Once a species is extinct, it is extinct!

As your life was, so will your future be. The end of all life does not mean the end of human life. It means the end of flesh, but not spirit. Spirit exists on all planes, and it is not definite that your spirit will be destroyed along with Earth. Earth is unable to replant itself. It cannot revive itself! Only man can manage to do that.

Never in the annals of life have so many people prayed—many are praying now. God has been despised and now is revered. In most of your religions God is seldom mentioned—only the names of God's greatest teachers are mentioned now. That is not to continue. God is a merciful teacher of teachers, but not You. You are of God, but God is not of *you*.

We are here now to seek out teachers. Teachers are always

here, but students have been seeking nonsense for so long that teachers have given up in despair. That is not to continue.

If you are the only ones who can save Earth, then let us begin. We will help! The Earth is not to be restored. It must be preserved. You must take immediate action to cut the destruction. Once that base line is achieved, then you can begin to preserve. Shore up the streams and rivers so the oceans are not polluted. This is the place to start.

Once the water is safe, your air is cleansed. The air is saturated with chemicals of many years, but it can be blown clean, if the water being drawn from the earth is clean. This is the best and easiest way to clean.

Now if that is the only way to insure clean air, why do you waste time? Begin immediately! The only thing left is the air you breathe. Once that air is too bad, you cannot be saved.

If you say, "I cannot clean the water—that is the work of the government," you will be lost. You are the only ones who can do it. The government is not of God—it is of you. You elect and protect them. If you destroy your government, it is not God—it is you doing it.

We watch you elect and reject men every day. Why do you do that? For what reasons do you elect them? Why are they good until elected? We sense jealousy. If that is true, you are all in the grips of hatred.

Hatred is now the worst crime you face. Anymore it is not

a crime to kill. You do not punish if a person hates others enough to kill them. That is a sin and will be punished by God. You are not hard enough on those who are evil. You let them flourish now. They are in charge. You are not strong and firm in your beliefs. You fear too much!

Fear is that which is in you that does not believe in God. You are so sure life is the way it looks that all you do is sit and watch. Your life is not the way it is because God created an atmosphere in which you could live and create. You are creators here! If you are not, that is your own fault. Never blame God for the fault of man. It is stupid to do that.

When you blame the other party, you blame yourself for not taking charge—which is why you are upset. If you sit and stare into space—acting like a robot, no one cares what happens to you. If you actively seek, the world helps. It is so.

While you seek, the work you do is fine and you feel great; but if that work is not appreciated by other people, you often cry. Why? Your work is yours and others are not your judge. Your judge is God.

God sits in judgment over all, but does not sit and watch. You have Guides. You have your own spiritual helpers who guide you through the maze of life. If you are in touch with them, they will help.

In the end, if you are successful, you reach the point where you cannot keep the human body any longer. At that time you can seek the next plane. That plane is easier than this one, but many often return to Earth to earn extra points—so to speak. These are the teachers. We are not referring to this latest pack of wolves that wrench money from you, but are not interested in teaching you or your children. We refer to the teachers who are sent to help you grow and prosper and be able to leave this plane. We will refer to them as *Spiritual Teachers*.

Spiritual Teachers are not always easy to find. They may be here today and gone to another place by the time you seek them again. Once you find them, you must always work hard, because they may leave.

If you cannot find a Spiritual Teacher, it is because you are not yet ready. You have more work to do. All of the work given to you is to be done before you seek more. This is the hardest lesson for many. Many, many prefer to sit and listen to Spiritual Teachers and watch them, rather than do their own work. The work is what frees you—not the teacher. Now if this seems too easy, try it!

In the world there are many who pass themselves off as Spiritual Teachers, but you will know. We never let you feel total comfort in the presence of those who might exploit you. We never let you become so still in your heart that fear escapes when you are in the presence of evil. We will never let you suffer at the hands of a charlatan. It is you who seek such people, not us.

If you need help, ask your Spiritual Guides for advice—then listen. In the work of *The Guides*, as we will call them, you are their only reason for being here. They exist and are created by

God. They live within You. Your life is lived with them. If you fear, they calm you. If you are angry, they cool you. If you are in love, they laugh with you. Your life is watched over. You are not alone.

If your Guides are never consulted, you live life entirely on your own; but the moment you decide to consult them, they will offer you help. It is always your decision! Never are you to blame your Guides. Your Guides are your guides. No way do they have the power to take over your life—what a ridiculous idea for some people to believe. That is impossible!

You are in charge. You have the power while in the physical plane to become exactly who you want to be. Your Guides are not powerful in the physical plane, but extremely powerful in the Spiritual realm. As you grow, we will tell you more about your Guides.

This has been a long session and our Scribe has work to do. We will be back and center you in God's work.

Chapter Three

The way of the world is now the way of man, rather than the way of man being the way of God. That is where the wrong road was taken. In the work of man is much that is deceptive and error-filled, but not in the works of God. If you are too deceived, you are ready for God.

The work of God is not your work now. Your work is not of this world, either. It is the work of your soul that needs you, not the world of work.

You are often misled by the media of your time to believe the world is a very interesting place—when it is not; and you are often led to believe you are the only one who is leading a boring life—when you are not. All of life is boring, if you are not doing God's work.

In the things around you, you can see a lot of misery and money has been achieved, but for what purpose? Once you achieve it, you often wonder why it is not important. The reason is—it means nothing to you spiritually.

If your life is not the way you want it to be now, you are the only one who knows that to be true. All others assume it is like it is because you want it that way, which is true. You change your life when it is no longer what you want. You do not change a thing if it is not uncomfortable.

Within the center of your being is a spot where you are You. That spot is either large or almost non-existent. It is how you relate to You that determines its size. If you let everyone else stand in front of you and take the light, and never try to advance, your spot is reflective of that neglect. If you push and prod to get into the light of God, your core is large and growing.

We are here to begin a class of new thinking that will lead to the discovery of You. If you are not interested, then you are not at all interesting to others. No one could be interesting if they do not know who they are.

It is so simplistic to believe you are an interesting person because you have money or fame. What a ridiculous idea! No one is interesting because they are able to perform and act over and over again. You are interesting because you are unique, different, and know exactly what it is you are doing at that time and place.

Now you can see it. The error in the ways of man is not the subject of this session. The subject today is: *How to be the rounded self.*

The rounded self is how you are when you exist on all dimensions and planes. You are not three-dimensional or four. You exist in all. We are aware this is not how you see yourself or others. You see a front, back, and side view—and not at the same time. You can estimate time and space, but not the degree of intelligence possessed by other people. This is the dimension we will explore today.

If you are intelligent, the world is a better place. Is that not what is said? Well, we see it as not true.

You are intelligent people—all of you, but few are internally able to construct a pattern that produced you which can be reproduced. That is our way of saying you are unable to predict the life of another, even if it is genetically the same as another—such as identical twins. You are not identical even if you look alike. That is the way you are outside, but does not reveal a thing about how you are inside.

As your life grows and prospers, you are too prone to forget that God is at the root of your being. You begin to congratulate yourself on being more intelligent than others. This conceit is what is at the root of today's war and games in the world of business. They are not happy at all by the time they finish working and go home to be miserable all alone.

This pattern is being developed as a suitable way of life for young people. Parents are encouraging their young to postpone settling down and raising families or being convent bound. They fear their life was harmed some way by not being free for a longer period of time before they settled into adulthood. This has been a disastrous experiment that is only now being recognized.

It will take another generation or two to really change this into a workable lifestyle. Now it is too degenerate to last. Those who espouse it are not able to reproduce by the time they are finally ready to settle their lives, and those who reproduce are the poorest specimens of the race. It is a genetic disaster that is harming the development of the entire human species.

If you are unhappy in the work world you built, we are not able to begin to tell you how to change it. We had no part in the construction of this elaborate façade meant to include all of society in a cooperative life work. It went along well for a few decades, but greed and sloth devoured that ideal. If you wish to be included in another program, you would have to decide among you as to what to do and how to proceed. In the meantime, all return to individual work.

We are here to help you gain your spiritual health, not your financial worth. If you are not making enough money, ask your Guides for assistance. They can always help you with that.

In this work we are here to help you fully integrate You into the world and put *you* back on the right track. If you cannot save the world, no one else will. All of the other planes have had a go at Earth, or will if it still exists, but you are stuck there for now unless you earn the right to move up the ladder. We are here to help you move upward.

In the future, if you are unable to change the way the world is moving, you will be without any place to live. The air and water are absolutely necessary to your survival. We do not need it. We are not of your plane.

This is the area in which so many of you sit back and let God work—or so you think, but it is not God's work. It belongs to you. You were given dominion over the Earth and all that is in it or on it, so you are responsible for maintaining the safety of the race—not God.

When the work of today is left to tomorrow, it is not done. It is ignored, and all begin anew. You are to begin today to finish all of the day's work before it is dusk. If you are too busy to finish by sundown, you are too busy. Act to eliminate any other work. No job is that big it cannot be done in a day. Your life is such that you space out work to last forever, and it is done poorly as a result.

You will begin to sense life is to be lived day-to-day, when you do your daily work each day. After the end of each workday, you are to be able to relax and meditate. This source of inspiration is necessary if you are to be *you*. Never meditating causes you to constantly stress the wrong area.

When you are in the White House, you will be in charge, you say if you are an American. But what does that mean? We sense a reluctance to take responsibility, the need to blame others for failures you have taken part in achieving. You are not the only one to be successful. You are only one entity among millions. You are necessarily in this together. No single individual is responsible for you or your families. You are the source of the power; and if it is not used properly, you can change the administration. You cannot change a person, though.

If you have ever tried to change a person, you know it is not a piece of work easily accomplished. It is a terrible responsibility to assume you know how such a person should be. If you are wrong, and you usually are, the consequences are so great your soul could be harmed. We suggest you never seek to intentionally change another person's thinking. Instead, let that person decide to be like you. No one will want to be like you if you are not ideal. There! You are not ideal, are you?

If we set out to settle old scores and take revenge on those who have hurt you, we would be causing you to be unable to return to Earth. This is not the role of Spiritual Teachers or your Guides. God is the arbitrator, not you.

When you are in the hot seat at the end of your life, you will see how it is to be hosted and toasted for doing a great job, or you will be punished. "It's not a big deal," you say. Well, if you have to come back to Earth to relive this life, we are not interested in being there. It is not a great way to spend eternity.

In the work of your hands, as we mentioned before, you are able to soothe the wounds of spirit inflicted by the world. If you are able to do the only work you know how to do, it is the only work you do. It is not necessary to be able to accomplish several different trades in one life, but it is absolutely necessary to be able to live.

When you are the only one on Earth, and you will be if you do not progress, the only thing left for you to do is meditate. Then it will be understood, and you will progress. Ridiculous to wait until then—don't you think?

We are here to help you seize this time and be all you were intended to be in the flesh. Why wait for the next life, and the next, before you get your act together? If you are not helped to overcome the limitations of the flesh, it is possible Earth will be destroyed and you are still living on it. If this happens, we will grieve for the lost souls, but it is not our way to let it stop us from helping. We will help you right up to the day the Earth spins off its axis and collides with another major body. You are the only one to know if you are seriously concerned enough to take charge of your spiritual growth to pursue a destination on another plane at the end of life on this one. It is your decision.

When we recently came to view the Earth, we saw it was not as blue as before, and we were shocked that air is leaking out of the crust of the Earth and evaporating into the atmosphere. You are not taking evasive action to prevent this from happening. You must do double work now if it is to be stopped.

We are not outsiders looking down on Earth. We are Spiritual Teachers who are able to step into any plane and view it. We are not threats to you. You are threatening the other planes, though. Now is not the time to lecture on how to save Earth. We have studied it, but have no concrete plan to offer at this time.

In the work of this world is a lot of deceptiveness and sham. It is not materialistic or concrete; it is ugly and wars are waged to seek peace—actually to seek pieces of others' property. If you war—then seek peace, it is not the time to fire bombs and light bonfires.

It is the wrong time for flames to consume wood. The dense smoke is clogging the airwaves and causing oxygen to be consumed that will soon be needed for humans to breathe. We suggest you quickly get used to coolness.

When the world was destroyed by ice, it was not long before the sun warmed it up, but this is not to be done again. Your work has destroyed the crust of Earth and hastened its demise. You do not care for the woods and forests. You do not care for the lakes, streams, and rivers, either.

You are concerned with property that fills your houses to overflowing. It is stuff no one on Earth is willing to give up. In the end, it will be overflowing and spilling into the lives of another type of being. If you cannot live on Earth, who can?

We foresee you becoming restive. It is a worry, but not yours. You will be long gone by the time Earth is gone, you say. Well, we have news for you. It is time to begin to flee!

This is the last of today's messages, and we are now aware you are able to see we are not harbingers of hope and good cheer, if you are unable to spring forth from this earth. Now we want you to meditate and fix upon a solution that will fix what ails Earth. If you cannot, we will help you flee.

Chapter Four

Your life is not over when you die. That is not the end, but the beginning. You will see this is the season of life when you go into another form and look back at this life to see exactly what went wrong or right and how to correct it or add to it.

In the fall of the year, you see leaves change color. This is the time when the chlorophyll is no longer used and color is drained from the leaf to reveal brilliance, if it existed, in the original leaf. If it did exist, the leaf is admired and perhaps even painted or pressed to preserve its beauty, but if the leaf is dead, dry and drab before its time, it is ugly compared to others. It is quickly raked and burned. This is quite an apt comparison. You will see more as we go forward.

Now is the time to prepare for the autumn of life, not when the temperature starts to fall and the days grow shorter. If you wait until then, the winter may advance too quickly and wipe you out. The work of your summer years is the work of health and vigor, and requires strength. The work of autumn requires mental stamina. The work of old age is wisdom.

It is never the time to start. There are always reasons why you can wait or why you should put whatever off until a better time, but when you first think of it—*that is the time*—after that is too late.

Once you are big, you begin to think of the world as beginning to shrink, and that the world grows smaller every day you live. If the world shrinks in size, what about you? You are not the only being on Earth. Only when you reach the years of wisdom do you realize that—and then it is too late to reach out. If you wait until the end, you are never able to reach out. Instead, do it as you grow. Take the hand of anyone who extends it to you, regardless of his or her skin or age.

If you are not the only one on Earth, who else lives here? We know you wonder about this, because you often ask this of your Guides. The others who exist on this planet are not the same as you. They use Earth as a laboratory. They spray the air for what you carelessly cast off that could harm them. If you try very hard, you can often smell it. It is a clean, sharp blast of ozone. After the air is sanitized, the others who share your space can once again gain strength and move more freely. Your disinterest in keeping your air clean has been a mystery to them.

If possible, please cease the fires. You cannot see how they cause the upper atmosphere to cloud and block the sun. If sunlight is unable to reach Earth, Earth will chill and freeze over before the next century is over. In that short time, all Earth will be forced to live on a very small area of land. Obviously, it will result in the death of many.

Whenever the air is clear and the sun is shining, all of life responds. Why not keep it that way? The rain clouds are not as dark as smoke. They dissipate into rain and wash off the crust of Earth. When rain is over, if Earth truly washed away its dirt, a rainbow is apparent. You are the only species who can enjoy rainbows, so enjoy and perpetuate their appearance.

What you see is not what is. The appearance of some thing or person is not what it is. You are not a form or shape. You are the collection of molecules representing the form or shape, but in spirit (not in flesh) *you* are You. You are a spiritual entity dwelling upon Earth in a costume that identifies you from everyone else. It is no different than a masquerade.

What you wear or how you look is your choice. If you like to appear beautiful—fine! If you like to look ugly—fine. It is your choice! We now see all trying to look different, operating upon their bodies and changing their faces, but it has no effect whatsoever, because they remain the same entity. If that entity sincerely wished to change, it need only start a lengthy period of meditation and contemplation—then such work would be substantial and lasting. Everything else is merely mutilation of the flesh.

In the work of the world exists a type of rhythm and rhyme heard on upper planes. The rhythm and rhyme is no longer very strong. It is disparate (perhaps desperate?) now.

Why are you slowing your work? For what reason do you now seek to end your duties? Were you unable to find agreeable work--still trying to end your work? If enlightenment is to be attained, it is absolutely necessary for humans to work each and every day while living on Earth.

If you cannot work due to injury or illness, it is your job to get healthy. You cannot let it go. Work on it every day until you are better or death removes it. Never sit still a day or two doing absolutely nothing. It signals the body you are ready to die.

As you grow and expand your work, all should benefit from it. If the work you do does not first benefit you, then others, it must be changed. You cannot spend your life doing nothing for You.

All work on Earth is not silly and inane. It is chiefly meant to occupy the mind and hands as Spirit grows, develops, and learns to manipulate the elements of this plane. If you develop only your body, neglecting the spiritual aspects of your life, you will be back!

We are here today to help you achieve enlightenment. We do not want you to return to Earth again. This is our opportunity to speed things up. It is the time to hurry you through this plane, before Earth is no longer receptive to human life. All work on Earth is not done, but now it must be. You will know when it is done. The world will be a joyful place when all know they will leave this plane at the end of this life.

All reading our words are capable of making this your final transit. We strongly urge you to do so. While you are here, and able to read our words, let us encourage you to do *something*.

Begin now to meditate more than you ever did before. If

you currently meditate in the morning and evening for a short time, lengthen the time. If you currently meditate during the day as you work, deepen it.

We can never get enough energy. In earlier times Earth had its own energy, but not now. It is unable to generate much energy. All is being used to birth new souls. If you continue to birth at the rate you are now, the world will be overburdened with so many immature souls that it cannot possibly control or provide for all. Even now you are reaping the results of this problem.

Never work on how to end life. Let life go. It ends at its own pace. If you succeed in helping people end their lives, it is God's work to put you in your place. We advise you to stop now. It is the will of God souls be birthed or die, not yours or ours.

All souls birthed are to die in the way of God, but not at your hands. You are not to kill. If you kill, it is a moral wrong that cannot be excused. It will result in your automatic return to Earth.

In the event Earth is no longer available, you would be returned to yet a lower plane—which would be most unpleasant. You are unaware of this? That is not true! You are totally aware of all you read here. It is written in the wind of Earth and totally surrounds you. All you need do is meditate deep enough to enter the beltway and gather all you need to know now.

If you could not work because it was not good for you, why are you still here? We suggest perhaps you are here to teach others. You are not as you were in the past, but you are great at it.

The teachers of spirit are being lined up now. The world has cast off many now preparing for their best role. They are studying, meditating, and working hard at spiritual tasks that will enable them to be of assistance to you and all others. You, in turn, will help them achieve their destiny.

While you reside here, and we above, the work of your hands is not used for the work of Spirit, but we suggest that in the future you will be able to use it for spiritual development, because the busier the hands, the purer one's thoughts. That is true of you all.

Wherever an idler sits, the grass is not green. Work of the hands is best if not done at night, because it is not as sharp. If you are the only one who resides in your home, you may design and plan your work for the day, but do not sit and work at night.

Your wall of spirit is in need of refurbishing. Insights gained in the evening need the light of day to insure they are not poorly designed and developed. If you work at night, it is best to sit for at least three hours and do nothing once you return home; that is the time it takes you to develop stamina to do your work—then stay awake for ten hours before you are due at your workplace. We see you understand.

In the work world there is a lot of damaging confusion now. It is not a great place. You need to redo a lot of your old work and reorganize the way it is done. As you do not care about the work of those who are dependent upon you for their daily labor, you harm many and help few. It is a great responsibility to be in command. If you shirk the work, you will pay a great deal for having failed.

In the work of the world, you are the only one to do your work. If it is not done, it is your responsibility—not the other person's. The idler who shirks work and expects others to do it will be cast off and given worse work. If work is not great, then change it! No excuse is accepted for bad work. You are only required to work, so do it and ask for no vacation.

Now, now, we are not saying you do not deserve vacations. We are saying you must earn them. If you are on vacation and deserve it, you still must work. However, it is not the same as your daily tasks. You are to relax, which is hard work for those who refuse to do it otherwise. Once you learn to relax, it is easy. You then work at learning a hobby or other pastime that helps you be the real *you*.

In the world of tomorrow you are not the only one here on Earth, but the only one having difficulty. You will not be allowed to harm others who live on this planet. You will have to make do with the remains of what you wasted. It will be quite a long time before trees and plants grow back and animals multiply enough that you may eat them again. All desert area will remain unfertile, so you are stuck if you do not know how to farm and ranch. The ways of God are not mysterious, but clear. You will pay for not maintaining what was freely given to you now.

The time has now come for us to sign off for this session. We can see the work of today is not as cheerful as usual. Since you are never to be gloomy, we are ending on this note: *Be careful of the dark and you will never be unable to see.* If you understand, you are enlightened!

Chapter Five

This is the time of the end, but the end is not in sight. The end is a long drawn-out time of dying and celebration. All who can, will be entered into the next plane—and all who cannot, will be left to forage. This is the fate of the damned.

In time gone by on your plane, all of this happened before. It happened when the area you know as Atlantis flooded, and all were taken. It cannot be like that again, because your world is not a peaceful one. It is too barbaric and cruel to enter the upper planes.

What is needed now is a leader and those who follow, then another leader and more followers, and another, and another. That is happening! You are all followers until you find someone who does not know and you show them the light, then you become the leader. Leaders are not rulers! Leaders merely show the way.

Never obey the rules of another, because they are not the way—follow your hearts and souls. While you seek the way, your life is stretched and pulled to overcome past resistance to authority, which is so evident in your lifestyle today. You must learn not to resist authority if it is directed toward saving your life or improving it. It is only to be resisted if it is self-perpetuating and useless.

Never seek out a man or woman to be your workhorse. Seek out a man or woman because they help you be the best you can be. That is why you marry and have friends.

When you are the only person in a group who believes in God, it is not difficult; but if all believe in God, it is. That sounds strange, but it is true. You cannot decide if your way is best or some other way is better when among many who believe they are right. That is what will happen in the days to come, but it is no real problem now.

We are here to begin a new world order of things to be done in order to prepare for the time when air and water are no longer available. You are to begin to breathe shallowly, then deep and shallow, and then deeper as the days become beige instead of blue. If the sky is brilliant and the sun is out, breathe deeply and continuously; but if the sky is not bright and the air is stifling, breathe cautiously. The oxygen in tanks is not the same as in the atmosphere, so be cautious of such extremes. You will be able to linger here even after oxygen levels are extremely low, but you cannot come back again for another try at Earth's lessons.

If you are unable to breathe, the air is unsuitable for development, and you will be unable to grow in God's way. God has never given anyone such a challenge. You did this to yourself. We will begin to work to free the souls of those who are endangered and unable to fully comprehend that this is the last life—and they cannot waste it!

In such places as Africa and lower Asia we will work through the religions in place. There is no time to seek out teachers there. The work is not as difficult if the people are poor. The work is much complicated by wealth and prosperity, such as in Europe, Asia, and the Western Hemisphere. The United States has already deteriorated from its former magnificence and will be out of control for a long time to come, because it is deeply affected by the air and water contamination it produced and then taught others to replicate. This time is coming fast.

You seek God when you cannot see your way through the mists of morning, and when you cannot seek help from others. As of now the mists rise to the heavens daily, but not for long. There will be much darkness over the land if smoke is not stopped. You will be colder than you have ever known. This is the time to prepare for the future. Stop the fires!

Get going on developing life that requires no heat to survive. Seek out the means to conserve and preserve food that requires no heat to prepare. In the end you will be able to heat yourselves as done in days of cave dwelling, but food will not be able to be cooked as it is now.

What is wrong now is that many have so much they cannot imagine life without money. They do not understand life existed before money and will outlast money. No money will save you if you are foolish. That is a lesson many learned, but many more refuse to take to heart. You cannot kill, steal, or forge currency to get money. It is always taken from you. If you need money, we are aware it manifests itself, but you are not to ask for what you do not need.

Imagine you are not wealthy and not well. If it is difficult to do, you are lucky. Many inhabitants of Earth do not know what it is to be wealthy or healthy, yet they have the best chance of survival.

The meaning of many scriptures of the Bible is now appearing to represent these times. The verses were prophecies meant to be read and understood at this time. Within the work of many wise and learned men and women of the past is the world you now approach. Seek out their wisdom and learn what you need to do. When that is done, all is up to God. You are unable to move forward.

God is the supreme judge and the only one to move any of us forward and upward. In the final judgment, if you are unable to move forward, you will be left here—then you will know what it is to be without God!

Never sit in the shade of a dying tree. It leaks sap and drops its leaves. You are to sit only under the trees of life, which are the trees you plant now. The old trees adapted to using more air and sun, and will be unable to grow in the rarified air of tomorrow.

Plant easily-trained plants and vegetables and let them grow wild. You plant vegetables in gardens now, and they are unable to fend for themselves. It is important to develop hearty species of vegetables which are capable of surviving on their own.

What you now lack in imagination will show up later as

scarcity of goods. You will then be unable to materialize what you once took for granted. Earth is not a manufacturer once depleted of its ores and you work all its organic riches out of its depths. You are the keepers of Earth and have despicably treated your ward as an evil stepparent might. Never again are you to be given such freedom.

What lies ahead on the next plane is not so much materialism as spiritualism. That is why spiritual people of this plane are now way ahead of many others. They can see into the next plane and know it is good.

What each person needs to do now is sit and meditate daily, but too few are willing to do this small thing. It is too much effort and requires self-discipline—two things now in short supply. We seek out those who are willing to help, and show their willingness by meditating daily. If you wish to be on the side of wisdom, we strongly urge you to meditate longer than you do now.

Wherever you are, God is also there. It is unnecessary to move to sunny shores or mountaintops to be near God. The Scribe is not from any such *power spot*, yet she works to prepare you for this message. She is not the only one. She is one of many working now to preserve Earth.

Earth is not a toy for you to experiment with and then get a new one. It is the only work entrusted to you; and if you cannot be trusted, it is the only work you will know.

What is wrong? Why do you seek news of the world, but

not the way of God? Are you sure you know it all? Why would you care if the rest of the world is not like you? Why would you think others should be?

The ways of God are many and the ways of man are not. The ways of God inspire and completely thrill you, but the ways of man are low, mean, and never thrill you. We will not let you see what man can do if it is not good. So why seek to know the evil men do?

Ignore the past and it will come back to haunt you in the future. You are the future. It is a time that never arrives. You are to the future what you are to the past—no difference. The future comes after today, but you never live in any other time but today. That is why you are always strongly urged to live NOW.

We are not afraid of you, but you are never sure of us. That is a strange paradox, since you are the only ones in power on Earth. All other entities are restricted in their movements and unable to manifest their work, yet you believe we have the power to make things happen.

Witches and warlocks are silly. You are not different, regardless of what you call yourselves. You are human beings sent here to work out tasks that will free your soul so it can progress to the next plane.

If you play at being God, you will lose this time and repeat the exercise. That is your punishment. You will in effect have to be reincarnated over and over until you learn you have no power if God does not grant you life.

When the world was young and struggling to build an ethical framework upon which to erect its highest achievements, the work of individuals was seldom seen as senseless, but the work of the masses was doubted. Today, single individuals are much more likely to be feared and doubted, whereas the ideals of the masses are cherished as folk wisdom. You need to look to your ideals. They are far from what you need in the years ahead.

While on Earth, we are here to bring you worthwhile ways to help out in the end. We are not here to hurt or harm you in any way. If you become frightened by our words in this book, we strongly urge you to seek out a wise person and confront the issues that scare you with them. If you let it go, it will change you and cause you to fear. Fear is not the answer. Fear is the enemy of man!

What is needed today is a world of peace and contentment, but it is not possible in the short time left. You will be unable to contentedly sit back and watch as others shorten life's reign on Earth. You will have to become actively involved in preserving your life. No more are you to give silly reasons for smoking, drinking, and constantly acting the fool. You cannot determine why you do these things, but it is obvious to others you are not in control. You are in control when you can stop such behavior at any time and not miss it.

We suggest you begin at once to learn control. Otherwise, you will soon be in a desperate state of deprivation. The strong will be able to move. The movers can escape for a time, but in the end, all is gone. You must prepare for that time and act accordingly. No one ever said Earth was a continual way of life. You assumed that because you carried no memory of the past with you into this life, but it is only a station along the way.

If you need to begin a new way of eating and drinking in order to prepare your mind for the trek, you should not begin immediately. Take time to visualize the trip and what you will need—then begin. We see many of you are fully aware and develop visualization skills, but others think it is magic. What rot! You are not stupid. Think! If you can think—and you can—then why not fully use that capacity?

We suggest you begin to meditate on when you will be able to designate exactly what you want to do and how you plan to do it. As you meditate, a picture will form. You need not prepare a picture and memorize it. It will appear. Once you see the vision of your life, correct, amend, and add on where you wish—only then can it appear.

Working hard is not hard. Idling is much more difficult. We see the masses trying to work now, but being disturbed by the higher strata who are not working hard. This is a troublesome business. You must rid yourselves of such idlers in top positions if you are all to work. No way can any organization exist long if idiots run it. That is now apparent, yet many continue to crow and brag about the achievements of today.

Why would you boast of putting millions of people out of work? Why would you see yourself being proud of a job if it produced nothing but toys? Your poison is all over the globe now. It is not confined to a few areas of your country. It is here, there, and on the rise in all cities.

In poor countries people are struggling to maintain their old religious convictions while earning a living, and they find themselves hurt by the conflict. You of advanced societies are not any better. Stress is so abundant in cities and the countryside that you all suffer—not just the overstressed. We will talk about this at another time.

When you can see, yet cannot see the way, all is lost. You must see the way first, then pursue it with all haste. To go forward rapidly without a plan is why you are where you are now—lost!

In the future of this work we will outline the way to place yourself in the very best position for you to develop. We will also plan a work for you to do. You need only continue to read and study our words as we do all the work. Once you thoroughly understand, we can leave you to spread the news of God's coming to Earth because we will not be here then.

Whatever you think, you are...
And whatever you are, you will be!

This is the end of today's session. We will take time to review what you now need to do for the sake of your soul.

1. If you are unhappy, it is no one else's fault. It is your way of life that is at fault. You must examine it and work out a plan to correct areas in which you are failing to perform well.

2. We are here to help. We are not here to lead you out of the Garden of Earth's delights and problems. You created them and continue to maintain them, so it is your problem.

3. We are here to insure that those who cannot see they are not alone are made aware of God's interest in their soul's development and desire to move them forward.

4. If you are unable to change, you will be changed. It is either your choice or God's. It will happen regardless of your status on Earth. You may be able to advance if you work hard, but it is your choice.

What you need to always remember: God is here and now, you are here and now, and we are here and now. If you are to grow in the light of God, now is the time to begin—not tomorrow or when you decide to move.

We are now through with this session and will begin anew when you can thoroughly understand all we have said thus far. Do not continue to read if you do not understand. In time you will understand.

If you are overwhelmed at this point, pause and take time to meditate and think through your life and how it is and how it can be changed. Do not go forward until you know who you are!

Chapter Six

Your life is never over! You live as long as you are—and you always are. This is no riddle. This is truth. The word of God is forever.

We are here to help you understand that wasting time on Earth is a waste of time. It accomplishes little, since this is a school. You do no more work here than anywhere else, but your lessons are of a different sort from what you are taught elsewhere.

We are here to help you sort through evils of early times and gain experience from the negative forces that exist here. Nowhere else in God's world does an image exist such as you have created of the '*devil*'. It is an image that grows and wanes, but always in Earthly civilizations. All of you are set on believing that good and evil exist and in constant battle over your souls. That is rubbish, but it is a life you choose. We are not interested in such childlike games, but if it is of use to you in absorbing the laws of God, we expend no worry over it. The work of *devils* or whatever is not of any concern to us. However, we do not care for such things to continue.

We need you to finally recognize God is all! You are only the work of God's hand, not the end of God's being. You will realize this is the only place in the universe without God at its center. You must correct this now! We can concentrate once this is done. As of now, the world you live in is such a confusing place for humans—and only human. It is not a place where other entities can come and go readily.

If you all want to blame God for the mess you have created, you better be prepared for God to clean it up. That is a sad day. What you do and say is you—not someone else. What others say or do is their business. You are not held responsible for the words or works of someone else, but you will be taken severely to task if you are not careful of your work.

We send you a little taste of what is in store if you do not listen and God sends angels to clean up Earth. The work of God is chastening. God is not calling you to clean up Earth. It is your place. You are now calling out and asking God to clear it of evil, because you blame God for creating it. That is totally wrong.

When the world was created for you, it was a beautiful garden of many plants and animals you were given the right to use as you saw fit. Over the years animals have been killed wantonly and plants uprooted and trampled. Never a thought when you did it! Never a doubt you were wrong! Never a care for what you killed!

Now all look sadly at what is left and cry out for God to clean up the world. Why? The world is yours. You are in charge. To call God is like calling up a dead ancestor and demanding an inheritance you were given—which is now gone and you want more. We are not implying God is dead, but you get the message.

Within the next few months *after* reading this, you will fear your life is over and God is coming to wipe out all on Earth, but after that you will no longer fear. We seek those who are afraid. We seek those who are concerned about the way the world is going and want to change direction.

We are here to help those who help others. If you never bother with neighbors or relatives, we know you will not help us. It is that simple.

Selfishness runs in families. It is this tendency to be like those who raise you that concerns us now. The family structure was the choice of your past, and today it is no longer used, but there is no other structure replacing it. What do you plan to do?

If the work of today is done today, what is there to do tomorrow? Well, that is the work of today. Today is always today, and tomorrow never is. That is the simple explanation, although you prefer convoluted, confusing definitions for all truths. Why?

If the work of today is today's work, then what is to be done tomorrow? That is what you are worried about now—and it is never tomorrow. Therefore, the worry of your life today is never done with tomorrow's work. You see how confusing it can get? Why confuse simple issues?

We are here today to talk about the world and humans' place in the next century—your time. We have no time, but you do. The world is now in its last phase, and it is not yet ready to die. We see you struggling to end this phase and begin the last one, but you do not know how to begin or end it. We came to help you *end the end*, but find you are not ready. This is a surprise, since you have talked about it for over twenty years.

Why is it so difficult to change? We surmise it is now not believed by the masses. When the work of a few is shunned, the work of the many is not great. The work of a few always leads the mass of population. It is the best way. You can see if it works before following through. This is the easiest way as well, but the easy way is not taken. The dark, rambling avenues are now closed and the broad boulevards are cluttered with bodies. The direction to take is anything but clear.

While on Earth, we are here to ask you questions so we can gain access into the hearts of men and women, but the answers are unclear. We seek clarity so life can be drawn into a pleasing design. If the design is not good, we help you change it. If the design is too complicated to follow and absorb, we help you simplify. But if the work of man is such it cannot be used, we cannot help.

Why are so many people seeking seers? We see it all over the world. The seer is no different from you in that the seer is also human. We are not.

We are here to help and confront you with your future. The work of man is not here. It is in the next plane, and we wish you to advance now. Why settle for this *life* when you can be free?

The work of a few in the world is pleasing and great, but many others work at disgusting and degrading labors they hate. They are unhappy and disillusioned. Their work is not good. We want you to strive to complete the work you have been given on Earth—and get out.

Many seek money, but money is not power. Power is what the rich prepared themselves to keep. Money is taken and wasted, but power can be saved. It can be wisely used, but is now wasted.

What is wrong? Do you fear power, or are you so interested in playthings and vacations that you cannot concentrate on the work at hand? We seek out those who work—and work with them.

You may seek our help. Work, work, work, we will see it and will come to seek your help. When we seek your help, you can do your work. It is easy once you have seen it in action.

Why does a scribe write for us? That is easy to explain. The Scribe writes because writing is her work. She writes, you read. We condense the material and seek a clear way to transfer it to print and she is the instrument. You are an instrument of God's work, too.

All are concerned with work. All is important that involves work. You are all the work you do. If you do not work, you will not move on. The work of the world is to work.

Why would you stand in line for a long time and not get a ticket? You would not do that, but many are standing in line and will not get a ticket to leave, because you are standing—

not working—not developing your talents. If you sit and stare, it is over. You might as well go on to the next life that will be here on Earth.

You cannot progress if you do not work at this life. You may not win the big prizes, but you worked. That is the way of this world. To win, you must work.

When the work of your world is done (and work is done), we can spot survivors. They stand out. You are a survivor. You are here, but you may not survive the next time. The work of Earth is almost done. It has been destroyed by past generations of people who cared nothing for you—and you care nothing for future generations, yet future generations will be you.

What is wrong on Earth? That is not easy to answer. It is a beautiful planet now endangered by its inhabitants. It cannot replenish itself. It is old and dying, and people are not worried. We are.

You should look at how you destroyed this home of yours. It is as though you thought it was of no further use to you, yet you all hate to die. Why would anyone create chaos at home? It is not a series of accidents; it is the carefully created work of many people that destroyed the home of all.

When you are the oldest inhabitants on Earth, and Earth is ready to slip out of its orbit, we will rescue only those able to move up to the next plane. We cannot nor will we be interested in moving those who despised us—and God. It is their time.

Why on Earth are you there? We are here, you are there, and all is correct. The end of an era is reached and concrete ideas are shared, but not now. Now all think they are individuals. No one thinks in the way of cooperative life.

We see you do not trust one another and hate anyone who has more. That is the root of all evil on Earth now, and we are hoping to stop it from growing further. It may be too late, but we are hopeful.

Why are you the only one to know us? You are not! We exist, but on Earth you think you are the only ones who exist. This is a very narrow way to think, and it is responsible for much that ails your world. Once you realize we exist, angels exist, and all sorts of other entities exist, the world is not so strange. We are not fearsome creatures, you are.

Within the world is a fever and rage that is now out of control and threatens to kill off many. It is rampant in the cities and will destroy life, but not enough are concerned. The areas unaffected do not care. They seek still further distance, but distance is nothing. The plague of death is upon all. The riots of cities and farmers are the same. The work of the factories and craftsmen is the same. The art of the painter is the same, whether it is on canvas or a large building.

The area you live in is connected to all other areas. You will be unable to escape responsibility for fewer and fewer lives being saved. You will be unable to lie about your part in destroying the world. You will be held responsible as many before you are now being sent back to live in their own refuse.

We will help only those who can refute the lies of the many.

What goes on now is not as bad as in the recent past, but the loss of life is. You are not to kill! We are aware of the need for bloodshed on a worldwide basis every so many days. It is a pagan idea. You are pagans! You do not recognize that God is not responsible for your life—you are!

Why we are here is of little use to anyone who does not believe we even exist or God is in the seat of all power and you are not. The woes of this world are now apparent to all other planes, and you will not be welcome if it is not clear you had nothing to do with it. How are you able to claim that? We suggest you start now to create a very strong case to support your claim.

When we are through, we will not belabor the point. We will leave, but you will still be here. Let us begin to understand that now. Once you do, it is all clearly the work of God and you will be able to progress. We are going to go forward to greet the new arrivals in the next plane, and we hope to see you there. If not, perhaps you can make the Earth last until you get your life together and *can* meet us in the next plane.

Wherever you are, we will follow until there is no more time. When the work of this volume is done, we will know whether or not to write more. If this work is not respected, why would more writing be read?

This is the total response to questions from this session: Go and live and die, but make sure it is done in the way of God.

Chapter **Seven**

Note: This session occurred early morning, November 7, 1993. Do you remember where you were that day?

This is the date of the world conference on the work of man. It is not celebrating the work. It is a day of mourning.

What is said here is not to be taken as a comment about You. It is the work of several different entities in the upper planes who are here to put Earth in shape. It is not the work of a *Super Guide*, or an angel, or such. It is the work of a group of Teachers of Guides—above the angels. We will not deny the truth of the Guides or angels. We are not here to begin a new order.

What you do now is of utmost importance. *You* have the power to choose. If you choose to ignore the messages being channeled to Earth by different sources, then you cannot deny at the end you chose to stay on Earth. That is your choice!

We are the only ones to teach. The others are here to guide or help in other ways, but we are teachers. We will not be as easy as the Guides or angels who are trying to steer people. We demand and call to your attention the wrongs. We will demand change. We are not pleasant if we do not like your work. The differences between Guides and angels are vast, yet you cannot determine it.

What if you had a list of chores to do, and it was not as good a list as you thought you deserved? You might think someone else's list was better or you had too much to do. The work of The Guides and angels is not like that at all. They both have definite work.

Angels are the only ones to be spoken of at the time of the world change, but they are not the only ones present. You want to know the reason? We are now here to teach you the difference.

Angels are now the worldwide choice for challenging the evil ways of man. People believe them to be human, but they are far wrong. Angels are not human. Angels seek out the great among you and tell them to begin war on the work of man, but they are *the warriors*. You will know if an angel touches you. It is not a soft stroke. It is a demand and a command.

What you are and who you are is determined by You and your Spirit Guides. We are not Spirit Guides. We are not even angels. We are the only group not on the plane where you now dwell. We are above and beyond the reach of this plane normally, but the Supreme Guide of us all has chosen us to help. We are being given a chance at change. We are not as into the ways of your plane as others are, but this is an asset. We can see more clearly the war and deceit.

What you need now is a lesson on who you are—not who angels are and who Guides are. We cannot understand why you are so into the work of angels when you are unable to do the work of man. We seek a lot of information from small groups, and we see them busily trying to be something they cannot be. This is not the time to begin a new religion or work out intricate plans for self-development. There is no time!

Air and water are not in abundance. You waste it on what is not necessary—*and it is*. Neither angels nor Guides can move you from Earth.

Your health is not important. It is the work of your spirit that counts now. Begin immediately to develop the way you are to be. If it is not done, you will not go forward. If you do not go forward, you will be returned to Earth—and that is not a fate you want.

What you are about to read is not the work of idealists or people. We are neither. We seek out those who are intelligent and capable of growth. We are resigned to letting all others remain on Earth. We are now seeking to help all men and women here at this time to develop to the point where they can take children with them. Children of the future are to be prepared for the end. They cannot all develop to the point of enlightenment before the air and water run out.

The world is not into the work of God, but God is into the work of the world; and we are here now to comment. The comments we make are not always understood, but you can understand that God is not pleased.

If you cannot move into the stratosphere or *heaven* (as you say), then you will be unable to leave Earth. It is a fate of great death and distortion of the soul. We are afraid many of you are not prepared for the sorrow. You are unable to comprehend death. If a friend dies, you mourn. If a family member dies, you go into limbo. If a parent dies, you seek answers. But the world is dying and you are not concerned.

Life is not a stage of development, as is often depicted. It is a plane. Planes are not piled one on top of each other, but the area in which you are is made up of a large number of planes. The place of one plane is the same plane as another plane. You are confused? We are now able to enlighten top scientists who can explain it intelligently—if not spiritually. Ask for their explanation, if that helps.

Not all of life, as you are experiencing it, is of use to your eternal soul. It is often merely a proving ground for new ideas. You cannot leave Earth, but Earth is now unable to support all your ideas. This is the challenge.

We are here to share with you the facts. The facts are not deep and mysterious. They are not to be shared with only a few select people. That is not God. The work of a few is not the way. We need all to help.

Within you is a heart and soul that beats as one. This is not clearly understood. You believe the heart is a pump that pushes blood from place-to-place, but it is the seat of your health. If that pump shuts down, it causes you to slow. If that does not slow you down, then the liver does its job of easing you toward death. The liver is the life of man. It is the center of your being. If the liver is not alive, you die.

We are not doctors or lawyers, and neither are required if

you live right; but Earth is now covered with those who are out to steal from others whose eating and drinking have destroyed their bodies. This has resulted in a huge growth of menial tasks that must be done if all are to remain civilized. We fear these tasks are not done. The work of medicine and law is not the work of people who are out to make money. Such people should be barred from that work.

When you can take up your work—and you do have work, we will be there. If you are unable to help out, we will help; but you will be expected to answer for why you were not ready.

Going to the top of the pile is not much of a challenge if the pile is not of God. The pile so many climb is made of dung. It is not worth a lot. We suggest you explain what you do to a child; and if that explanation is hollow and sterile, change it to the work of a dynamic, unique person who has much to be proud of and cares much for others—then you will be free.

Wherever you go you will be full of health and wealth. If you are unable to be of worth, you are unable to be wealthy. The law of wealth is the law of health. It is not known? You really are not thinking if you do not know such simple basic truths.

What you need to do to be wealthy is work hard every day, get along with your fellow man, and hurt no one. Remember? Within this simple framework is the stuff of life. If you are unable to complete this simple lesson, you certainly cannot go higher.

The work of the few does not free the many. Each person has to do his or her own work. The work of others does not translate into your area or transfer its power. You are not working to please others. You work to please God and yourself. If you do neither, then you are not a success.

Welcome to the real reason you are here. You are here to develop into a person who can speak, write, and learn. You are all given this opportunity, but many reject it early in life. That can be tragic, but the time to learn is always present. Life can be changed. Learning never is a pain. The teacher may not be good, but the lessons are.

If you have not learned to comprehend a language, you are handicapped. This handicap is far more damaging than a physical handicap, because it implies you do not help yourself. The physical handicap was not chosen, but lack of education is your choice. You cannot speak of life as being the choice of others. Your life is your life.

Having to be reminded constantly of why you are here is not wise. You need to ensure you will not be forgotten. If you are not careful, all of your work done over a long time could be wasted. If the work of many lifetimes is not saved, you will be sent back to start at the plane below this one—and that is not a good thing!

Without energy is our Scribe. We are taking a lot of power from her, and she has not been prepared for such a task. If you need to be able to take your work further, you need to develop the ability to transform our power to your body. This is not easy, but it can be done.

Place your hands on your head. Do you feel power? No. Your head is not transmitting. The heart and liver are the seats of your physical well being, but they do not transmit power, either. The power is being transmitted by the energy field that is You. *You* are not flesh. *You* are energy.

Pulling out the stops to get into shape physically is not wise, nor is it wise to jump into spiritual work. Take time to warm up, then begin the long series of workouts required to build yourself up. The power of the universe is not what goes into you. The power you receive is not from other parts of your soul.

You are a very powerful entity. The entire entity—your soul—is the product of God. Without God you are unable to enter the next plane. You must develop until you can take the infusion of power and turn it into another form.

We can seek out those who have been developing themselves over the course of their lives. If you try to jump into spiritual work, we watch to see how long you intend to work at it, before we commit ourselves to you. You get exactly what you seek.

Some of the classes we have seen on this plane are so silly and inane that we laugh, but you all are serious. The work of God is not silly and inane, but you can laugh. The work of God is not as you think. We are never as you are. We think of things we need and want—and we get them. You must construct, since you exist on a material plane.

The world is not as busy as it was. Why? Are you all sure you know exactly whom you are and why you are here? That is not how to progress. You must question. Ask for help. Go to the top of your education level and strive to push it higher. If you cannot find a teacher, we are always available. You need only ask.

Running into the wall of fate is not a truth. You are not running. You do not have a wall of fate, either. The fate of your soul is the work of you and your Guides. If you call for angels to help, you get angels. If you call for Guides, you may get angels.

Guides are now on Earth for the first time. The work of Guides is not to begin until the last drop of water and the last air is gone, but they prepare the rest to move now. The Higher Guides are not the only ones now pulling up people. Angels are helping. The effect of the angels is that they are more dynamic and dramatic. The Catholic Church has always recognized them. Those who are not Catholic are just as put off by talk of angels as Catholics are put off by talk about Guides.

The religious training of men and women is often why they are unable to seek God. They are not prepared to take charge of their lives. We are not here to condemn religion. It is necessary. It is important to teach an ethical standard. If you do not, then anarchy is bound to occur.

Within your mind is the cause of all your problems. You are not as you think you are, yet you become what you think, which causes comfort and distress. We are unable to think for you. You are the only one who does that for you. It is like trying to hire another to do your work; you will never be satisfied with how they do it. In the future you are not to go after anyone else to do anything. If you do, you will instantly feel stressed.

We are not here to demand you live as decent people. That is the result of right living. We are here to ask you to be the best you can be. If that is not your desire, you will be back— but you know that!

Work is not as hard as it appears to be, but your work is not the work of others. They are unable to do it, and you cannot do their work. So why are you always watching what others do? This preoccupation with what others have and do is unwise. It results in dissatisfaction or worse—smug conceit. Neither of these traits is worthy of men or women.

God has no war with you, but you war with each other constantly. The major wars are of no real worth. The minor, daily, ongoing conflicts are the real danger. You are unable to find peace.

When you die, you will know why this is the worst of all possible places to be. It is not the place of damned souls, but close. The old ways are still here, and the new ones are not apparent.

You are behind in your classes and now silent. We expect more noise and more enthusiasm about God. Once that occurs, all begins to move. Without delay we go now to prepare the next lesson.

We are not interested in what you do, but it is of interest to your Guides. In the future, we suggest you tell them before you do something. That way you can get input into the best way to be.

Work until we meet.

Chapter Eight

We are here today to escort you through the maze. You are not the only beings on Earth, but you are the only beings who are unable to correct your lives. You are upsetting the rest of the scheme of things for other beings who also dwell in your space and time, so to speak.

If you are the only beings alive, you are not the only ones who are angry about the way the world is being treated. The world of your creation is now the path of least resistance for everything. You do not care for the basic instinctive desire to be free or to be clear of all debt. This is a strange way to be, but it is the choice of your people. All over the Earth the work of your hands is being put aside so money can be made from money—and money made from money is worthless.

When you are the only ones left, we will be unable to instruct you in the ways of God. God above is not here on Earth. God is able to be everywhere always, but this is your realm. God does not expect to be involved, but expects his word to be kept.

Your policies are human—not divine. Your laws are legal, but seldom moral. Your morals are almost nonexistent now. The way of your flesh is the way of your mind—not the reverse, as it was in the past.

For a people who pride themselves on being in tune with the world, few are. We seek a tune and find none. What is wrong? Why is the world so disharmonious? Are you all afraid? Do you all seek the day you are no longer here? That is the appearance.

When the work of a few is suddenly seen as being the only work all can do, you are indeed in deep trouble. The trouble is not so much keeping busy, but that you are not content. Work is not the same for all people, yet it is the same spiritually. We may have confused you. Let us say this: Work is not necessary for the body, but it is necessary for grounding your spirituality. We sense a distinct desire to skip the hard stuff, so life is easy, but it does not work that way—*ever.*

Within a week of any one reading this material, we seldom expect a person to change, but if you do, you are good. We can see you. We know you are serious, and we will help you.

The work of Spirit is difficult, but not impossible. The work of your heart and hands is joyous and frees Spirit. If the work of your heart and hands is not joyous or freely given, we cannot develop into the soul of our true worth. That is why you will never be able to leave Earth, if you do not work hard every day. Once you master that lesson, as well as the other lessons, you may progress to the higher planes and eventually may even become a teacher much like this panel of teachers. The choice is always yours—not ours or someone else's.

Chapter Nine

We are here today to tell of the new work you will be doing in the years ahead, in order to prepare for the end of this age and the beginning of the eighth day. The eighth day is the way we refer to the next age.

In the last days of this world, we are here to help you return to the work of God and forget the world you created. To forget the world is not a big step, but for many of you it is not easy. You have placed your souls in jeopardy over the amount of money and material goods you accumulated. In the future, you will never again be able to accumulate.

This is not the work of a devil or demon. The ways of God are many, but humans often like to pretend God is not as powerful as God is. That is blasphemy! Prepare to die if you continue to imagine beings as having as much power or even more power than God.

The old days of your society were limiting and dreadful for women, but the new days are not much better now. Within only a few years you have reverted to the unsophisticated and wild ways of frontier times. You are acting like you are cowboys. You carry guns and rifles. You hint at living off the land, but continue to eat barbarously with your fingers and hands covered with food. Your lives are not enriched by the money you earn, instead many more are impoverished.

Since you do not care for sophistication and are unable to eat and drink daintily, we will cut up your food for you and feed you bite-size tidbits of information suitable for good digestion. Words that are too long or you are not literate enough to understand, we will write in monosyllables and short sentences in order not to distort the meaning of our words. It is not easy to reduce huge volumes of wisdom and distill it into small servings, but we are trying to do that.

If at times we sound a bit testy, it is because it is difficult to sit still and let someone ruin a work of art. Earth was the most beautiful of all the planets. It was the one on which all wanted to experiment. Now it is showing signs of wearing out and hurtling itself out of orbit. You are responsible—not us! We grow impatient, but you do not. It is this type of irresponsible behavior that casts us into deep despair, which we are trying to work out of now in order to save Earth.

The work of your hands is not to be despised. You do not appreciate work of your hands enough. When it is time to end your life on this plane, the only thing left is the work you did with your hands. Ideas are unavailable for others to study—only the concrete work you did remains. If your entire work life is spent working on paper or computer screens, your work is not appreciated. It is not seen. We suggest you begin immediately to build something.

When a person decides to build, it is the best time to begin analyzing the work to be done. Do not wait until materials are assembled and plans drawn up to decide what you might be doing wrong. Concentrate on the many ways the project could misfire—then think of its uses. If the negative aspects of the job outweigh its uses, we suggest you try something else. The work you do should not require a lot of pain and misunderstanding. If it does, you are in the wrong area of endeavor.

For a woman to become the best at what she does, it takes time to shed the duties of motherhood, housewife, and daughter, but it is best to wait until all such responsibilities have been met with a cheerful heart. No woman who waits is ever sorry.

Men do not have the emotional responsibilities of women now, but they are just as compelled to provide necessities as women. They work in the material world, while women work in the spiritual world. This is not a putdown! Women are wise and men are physically strong. To say otherwise or to wish otherwise is the worst sort of misinterpretation of the role of humans yet to be perpetrated.

Men are not to be respected for not providing for children and their mothers. Men are to be respected for doing what is required and doing it well, without caustic remarks. But if the man is not happy, we see no harm in his leaving for another woman, if he can provide for all. No woman really cares for a man who leaves her, if he provides for her and her offspring. This is not immoral and not a plea for divorce. It is the nature of man and woman. Arguing otherwise is a waste of time and cannot produce anything of value.

If a woman and man are not married and are not in love, it is not wise to be sexually involved. Sexual involvement is the root of love and will result in one of the two being harmed. Since a rule of passage to the next plane states clearly you may not harm another person, you can see such loveless sex can easily lead to a mortal sin that will prevent you from entering the next plane. Since that is why we are here, we will not condone the idle ways of drunkards and others who seek sex as a power trip. If you do, then mend your fences and seek out those who have been hurt and apologize.

Your life is your life, but it is not as complex as it was. When all on Earth were into the realm of single marriages with no divorce, the demonic, fiendishness of some men and women was beyond God's patience. The ways of Earth are not the ways of any other plane, but the outcome is transferred to all other places and times on this plane. If you cannot have a single marriage, then be done with it, but do not harm anyone as you end the relationship. This often takes a little more time than if you rushed and hurt others, but it is always best to take time not to hurt anyone else.

If your life is so difficult you cannot get through it, you can ask for assistance. The help comes in the form of an aspect of You. This aspect is often referred to as a 'Walk In'. Walk-Ins are not other people. They are You. You are multi-dimensional. (We cannot find a simpler term.) If you were only a single unit, your deep-down wishes would kill you; but since you are multi-dimensional, your wishes can be carried out to their end without ending your life on this plane. This is a very deep subject, and we realize many of you do not know physics, so we will try to explain it.

When you are born you have a mother and father and possibly siblings. As you age and live, the people in your life change. As they leave you and others enter, you fear change may harm you, so you dream of ways of being with them. Your dreams go forward as though you were actually living them, but you are not. You continue to live this life. After a time—maybe soon, maybe not—the dream episode ends and you resolve the problems of separation. The new *you* is a product of this resolution of dreams and separate existences.

What you need to do when asking for help from your Spiritual Guides is to request exactly what you need—not just an idea. The more explicit you are, the more exact the outcome. If you ask for help and help is not present, the reason is you are not asking for help in the proper way. The proper way to seek assistance is to ask aloud in a firm, cool, passionate voice for exactly what you need. If you need money, ask for an exact amount; later when you get it, always use it for the purpose for which you asked. Also, once a prayer is answered, remember to give thanks.

Too many of you never thank God for anything! It is such a vulgar display to see humans asking, asking, asking, and never thanking God for anything. You are not entitled! You were given a body to keep, a family to raise you out of infancy, and skill to make a living. What you do with those gifts is up to you. Any other gifts are entirely at God's discretion. Many gifts are bestowed daily on those who thank God for all they have.

Within a few months of reading this material, reread it again. In the meantime, let the words sift through all the material you read, and let the new interpretation alter the way you see the old material. If you cannot do this, then it is too advanced for you. Pray for added strength, and we will send you material you can understand.

Never sit and stare at a page of words. If the words are not interesting, let them sit while you work on another area. If you are unable to understand something, ask others. If they do not understand, then you are not associating with people of your own ways and should begin to seek out new associates. Often you are raised in homes that are safe havens for the young, but provide no nourishment for the advanced soul. That is no fault of the parents; but if you disturb them and hurt them for not being able to supply all your needs, you could risk mortal sin.

God is the answer...
Now ask the question

Wherever the mind flows, the body will carry you there, but the body can also carry the mind. If the body is upset and hurt, the mind aches. If the mind is upset and emotions harm others, the body is often attacked. Be careful of upsetting conditions.

We never seek you, but the work has developed to the point where you are now able to seek us. This is the surprise we have been waiting for: You are not all without sense. You are not stupid. You just do not like to work.

Meditation is not the hardest work on Earth, but many avoid it as though it was. Why? Is it because you fear something will take you over? We have heard that expression and we laugh. To be taken over by another entity requires the full cooperation of both parties and weakens both.

Why would you think someone in another form would want to be in your body? Your body is not the best vehicle. The entities of Earth are not without beauty of their own, but the entities of higher planes are very brilliant and powerful, and require the most carefully prepared bodies to be able to enter and speak. Without a lot of prayer, no soul is going to be the vessel of God. The words of God are not given to fools. If you are such a fool who believes you may be taken over, dream on and on. It will never happen.

In this session we have covered a number of questions which rise from the world's lips daily, but the world is unable to ask the right questions. In future sessions we will enter into the world's work and ask you what you need and want. Once we can work cooperatively and in complete harmony, all is better for Earth.

Much of your material on Earth is not of the Earth. You often sing songs of another plane and dance to tunes within your head which come from faraway times. If the dance you do and the song you sing is not of Earth, then where is it from? Let us say you know it, because it is already within you. Your life is preprogrammed, but you are always capable of making alterations and changes that affect the final outcome.

You come to Earth to learn a lesson and advance your soul. Once on Earth, you often forget you are here to learn. That is why the criminal mind is difficult to train. The mind is not readily able to accept a new idea; and if the mind has been involved with certain ideas for centuries, it is not easy to reprogram.

Where the old meet the new, the old are the more powerful. If the new can challenge the old, they may make progress, but it is very difficult. The old, old souls who were once dominant on Earth are leaving, so younger souls are now dominating the realm and are not prepared for the responsibility. If all the old souls flee, the remaining souls will have a difficult time, since there will be a void of leadership.

Many on Earth are now leading double lives. Half of their time is involved in earthly pursuits and the other half preparing for the end. These people are wise. We seek them out and watch them worry over the Earth, but they are not in the majority. We hope to help them with our lessons and books. If you are one of them, please ask us for help now. We will help you lead.

Whatever work you do, whatever time you spend on you, whatever fruits you harvest, this is the time to prepare for the best of times to be followed by the worst. When you are ready, that time will arrive.

Without a doubt, the only one who cares for you is your Spiritual Guide or Guides. Some souls have more than one

Guide, due to the many lives lived by some people. The more lives a soul has lived, the more Guides. We are not Guides. We are on a different plane and have different responsibilities. If your Guides ask you to do something, you are not compelled to do it; but if their elders—the High Guides—ask you to do something, you better be prepared for renewing your dues if you do not follow their instructions.

Guides are not angels. We see many on Earth are now confused about this. We hear the work of angels discussed on airwaves as though they are movie stars or celebrities. Angels are not human! Angels are God's warriors—and messengers. If you are ever asked by an Angel to do God's bidding, you best do it!

Within the realm of angels and archangels are many other vibrations, but they are not listed on a chart and distinguishable from other entities on that plane. We are not going to list and describe angels and archangels, nor should you. Angels are far above you, and God is not to be placed beneath them. You are not to call angels!

When the work of a multitude is not worthy of God, the work of a single person is not worthy, either. It is the work of a single good person multiplied by many that is of greatest worth. Are we confusing you?

Many different entities are working out of the way on the Earth. The most common entity known to man is the knowledge of man gathered in the past and still residing within the memory of each soul. This *past life*, as you may call it, is in the memory trace and is never destroyed. You can review knowledge from the past, but why do that if you do not intend to use it to further the work of God?

We do not condone doing *past life regressions*, because of the ego trip it gives some. We seek only the positive aspects of your soul's past when we ask for your help. We do not want negativity to be permitted to erupt—which is possible.

Why you do the funny things you do is not of interest to us, but we are much concerned over the flaunting of the old ways. Many are making money exploiting the wise ways of women—and many of them are men! This is not to say men cannot learn the ways of wisdom, but they must learn their lessons first before preaching to others.

In the past all the worries of humans were looked upon with no interest, but we are now concerned. We realize many of you have been aware for centuries that life has not progressed, that you are not as wise as you once were, and that the work of the past is lost. We see now that you are right. We will help you reclaim the past and use that wisdom now to raise your soul to the next plane.

While the time is not ripe for you to begin practicing the old ways, we are preparing you to use them. When you hear of the old ways, you will know. We are going to help all learn how to use the old wisdom to gain access into their past, so the next plane is no big deal. We will be back.

Chapter Ten

The work of today is not the work of yesterday or tomorrow. It is different. You have all around you NOW, but you constantly think of the past or future—which is confusing you and us. We would like to see you stop and think only of what you are doing and not concern yourself with other times or other people.

It sounds easy to us, but apparently it is very difficult for humans to mind their own business. The words of your world are always directed at others. Seldom do you tell yourself you are to work. This is the prime difference between spiritually-oriented people and those lost to the world. If you think only of others, you are not true to You!

In the work of God (as well as work for man) you think of others, but in a far different light. You contemplate the good of *all* men, women, and children—not just one person. When a mother teaches her children, she is not being self-centered or proud, she is doing her job. If the job you are meant to do entails teaching others, you are required to spend your days thinking of others; but spend your outside hours developing *you*.

We are unsure of the consequences of neglecting *you*. We are aware that the hatred of others is rooted in this—as well as jealousy. If you do not control you, and never think of the end product you will give to God at the passing over of your soul, we surmise you are in danger. The danger is not from anyone outside yourself, it is from within *you*.

In the beginning of your world everyone decided to be of the same color, but soon it became apparent you all had different ideas of what constituted physical beauty, and changed color. This change of color is only skin deep, but it is the final demarcation line related to all matters of personal integrity today.

We find it sinful that you might care that much about the size or color of a person. What does it matter if the heart and soul are pure? No one reading this book can say with true sincerity and humility that you are unafraid of another, which is not God's wish.

You are not to fear...
Fear is the enemy of all people!

In the work of your hands—not God's, we see the way of the world is to condemn those who worship. This is not the way of God, obviously. The worship of God in all its many forms is to be continued and never interfered with. We had great hope for the New World, but it is now as bad as the Old World—if not worse. Seldom has the work of man caused God as much concern as it is now. The anarchy and disputes over religion grow with each day—and no one is in charge.

Are you happy in all of the work you do? Do you see others happy, too? No. We know you are always afraid of what lies ahead of you. Your faith is disturbed, and you fear for the world. It is not our intent to increase your fear. We are here to challenge you to grow and develop, and clear the air and water so life may continue here.

Within you lies the solution to all problems. We cannot actually change a thing. We have no power on Earth. You are the engineers of your own fate, and only you have been given that power. God has the only word, and that word is get busy!

Wherever you go or wherever you would like to go, the work of man has already destroyed much of the habitat. You have carried litter to the mountaintops and the deepest crevices of the seas. It is a disgrace to see how many animals and plants have been destroyed by the careless turning over of earth. You turn earth, because it stands in your way or because it is not pretty, but you destroy layers of topsoil, as well as plants and animals that keep the crust intact. The crust of the Earth is no longer solid. It is loose and capable of washing or blowing away. This was a very stupid way to handle your planet. We see you understand.

When the world was first conceived, *The Teachers of the Upper Planes* saw it as a course in dominating and controlling the nature of spirits who feared God and needed to develop a sense of self. This is the only reason we care to continue work in this classroom now.

If you do not rid the Earth of its problems, this planet will no longer be habitable and fit for students. This is a serious problem, because there have always been other entities who reside on Earth, and they graciously admitted humans to their worlds. They will now be punished severely for having helped you. This is not to be forgotten. It is not the time or the place to concentrate on the other entities that reside on Earth, but at some later time we will answer those questions in depth.

People need to begin now to sort through their lives and decide if they are ready to advance or not. If they are ready, we are here to help. If you are not ready, we will let you fall. We are not being evil. It is your choice.

The world is not a nice place to raise children, and we concur with that deeply disturbing conclusion. You are not taking enough time for your children that almost any animal takes with its offspring. What do you think will happen to them? Do you expect your child will grow by itself? Do you think a child is capable of knowing about people and how to adapt? Your ideals are not ideals now. They are merely self-serving goals that are not acceptable to The Guides.

We are here at the request of your Guides. So many of you have not called or talked with your Guides for years and years, yet they are responsible for your spiritual growth. When you die (as you say), you are asked to explain the reason you are not ready to progress to the next plane; if the reason is due to spiritual deficiencies, your Guides are taken to task by The High Guides. It is their responsibility to help you, yet they are not permitted to interfere in your world. It is a difficulty now being attacked through meditation circles and groups all over the world, but many are still not in contact with their Guides.

As you grasp the meaning of why you are here—and you always have Guides to help you complete your tasks, you will see there is order and reason to all that is—and you are never alone. Angels are the servants of God, but not of man. Your Guides can and may call angels to help them, but you are not high enough to do that. You are being inconsistent, if you call upon angels, but not your Guides. If you do not know your Guides, you cannot know an angel!

We do not complain. We are unafraid of the inconsistency of your teachings, but we are very concerned you do not fear the deeds of man. You look for devils and demons, and there are none. The devils and demons in your world are people— not spirits or other entities.

If you set out to do wrong, it is fulfilled. That spark of malicious intent has its own life. Once it is free, it lives. It is not human nor spirit, but it has power. Its power is not as great as yours, since you produced it, but it has the power to harm anything weaker than you at the time it was created. You are to be damned if you set forth any of these *entities*. It is your work—not God's work that increased the misery of mankind.

When you encounter a *splinter*, which is what we call such an entity, you should disarm it and cause it to rejoin its original soul. This is not hard to do. If it appears to be haunting a place, tell it the soul has died and gone beyond and it is to join it. You need never fear such an entity, since it is lost and confused and will go wherever directed. It is a blessing to all who free such *souls*.

Not all splinters are *dead*. Most of them appear to you to be alive, but they are not true or well-developed entities. If you find yourself compelled to be with someone who is incomplete and destroys or disturbs all around you, you are probably witnessing the manifestation of a splinter. It is not to be permitted to take control. Quickly and quietly put such an entity to flight. Drive it out of your mind. Speak over and above it to change the course it is trying to compel you or others to follow. This is often all that is needed to rout the splinter. In time the splinter is absorbed back into the original soul, and that soul is held responsible for all it did while loose in the world. Again, this is a deep subject that requires more discussion than we are willing to give it now, but we will return to it at some later time.

If your life is not going your way, seek a new direction. Stop and look at all you have accomplished, then prepare a list of all you hope to do in the times to come. Once you are clear on how you wish to live, it is simply the art of living that takes up your time. You can polish and perfect it, or you can neglect it and reap nothing. It is always your decision.

The fact that you are always in control of your life is very disconcerting to most of you. We wonder why that is? If you had not wanted to live on Earth, you would have been spared this experience, but you all asked to be here. If you asked to be here, then why are you so sure it is the worst place to be now? The Earth is not going to change YOU. You change *you*—

nobody else can. For the same reason, you cannot change another human.

What you see is not what is. What you see is the impression of spirit on matter. The impression is often blurred by makeup or cosmetic surgery, but the true nature of the person remains. You need only look closely.

We are unconvinced that you entirely understand the gravity of your situation on Earth. It is often discussed, yet nothing concrete is done. We will be unable to help you change the ways of pollution and disturbance to the balance of the waters, but we can lead you toward the best solution. If you need help, you need only call us and the upper planes will research and develop the best ways to clear up the mire and contamination; but we have our own work to do and will not help if it is not requested and appreciated.

If this sounds a bit far-fetched to you, we call your attention to the work of Einstein. He is not without peer in your world. He is one of hundreds of learned seers who tried to prevent the work of man from ruining Earth, but he sought to identify the meaning of life as a way of dispelling ancient superstitious beliefs. Your scientists are unable to quickly decipher the meaning of his work, because they have no spiritual basis from which to deduce the entire cause of life and the realms around you. Anyone can understand Einstein's theories and still not be accepted by the High Guides as having sense.

You can now deduce how life began and will end, but will this change *you*? If you are unable to change, why are you so sure others can? We see you feel slightly uncomfortable when it gets to the point where you are expected to contribute. You deny this now, but very few have ever visited a stream and cleared it of debris or scum, yet this is the easiest of all things to do to make a difference in the water and air.

Why wait until you get organized? Why sit still while others pollute and endanger your skies? Is it because you are afraid others will laugh? They are scared, too.

When one person decides to change things, it is interesting to see the change in that person. It is a growth of such huge proportions that we are in awe. No one on Earth has grown more than The Scribe, yet The Scribe is far from done growing. You will see that as time goes forward.

We are not here to discuss any of the changes. We are here to inspire you to perspire and do what is necessary to save Earth. In the work of your life we see you often omit working on your spiritual self. It is as though it does not count. Why would it not? It is the single most important work you do!

In the work of your next life we will be unable to discuss the work of this life. It will be over. You carry forward only the impression of this life—not the actual events or circumstances. If this life is one of wealth, you will retain such a feeling. If this life is one of challenge, you will feel compelled to seek action then. The reason so many are unable to act now is because in previous lives you acted at the behest of others—not on your own. You now sit and wait for someone to tell you what to do. This is stupid! May we remind you? You are in charge! None of you has it really rough or is caged for life. The whole world is free.

You remind us that some people are not free now, but we assure you they are indeed free. No one on Earth is unable to escape from the place of their birth if they desire to do so. The way of the immigrant is the way of all people in the past. In your present society it is not the way of all people, but it soon will be. You are all about to be evicted. It may not be in your present life, but if you keep returning to Earth, it will be here shortly.

What will happen when you cannot live on Earth? That is the question you must constantly ask yourself. What will happen to those left on Earth? We can now see that you understand in your own way and in your own thoughts. It is a bit cynical of us to believe you will do nothing anyway, but that is where we are now.

If all that is needed is the work of a few, you do not have to do anything. Unfortunately, this work cannot be done by only a few. It requires the efforts of all. No one lives alone! You all drink and breathe. If you do not breathe, is it someone else who dies?

Now that we have made a slight impression on your mind, may we ask you to be aware of people who have no mind? There are many here on Earth for the first time. They are new to this society and the ways of the world. If you are not new, you are responsible for helping them grow and develop. However, that is not the point we are here to make. We are here to stop the destruction of Earth.

As teachers, we know you must repeat a lesson many times before it is acted upon. So if you feel you are being constantly bombarded by the same message, it is because you are a little quicker to learn than others who take longer. It is not enough to understand—you must act!

In the course of this work, we see you growing in the ways of The Guides now. You are aware, perhaps for the first time, that you are not alone and are expected to seek help, if you need it. This is a very important turning point for many of you. It is the time when you return to God.

We are happiest when you choose God. It is not necessary to choose God, but you will. The end of life is not the world's end nor is it the end of You. You live and grow toward the light—and the light is God. Never seek the dark. It is a waste of time and will only result in your being returned to Earth.

You ask: Who would seek the dark? There are those of small stature and weak minds who often gain power over much larger beings. It is their sheer determination to be someone that causes others to let them ascend to power over them. This is sometimes the case of spiritual types, too. They are dissatisfied with being human. They seek to be gods. This is the ultimate blasphemy and results in a diminished soul. You are not long in this plane if you decide to follow the path of such a leader. Your life is not permitted to continue. You are shunted off into a lower plane—and the lower planes are not pleasant. Enough of this!

We are here to help you start a program of relief for Earth. We are here to design a place for the entire human race to continue to live. We are here to help you grow in the ways of God, so you may move up into the higher planes *as time goes on.*

Time does not exist anywhere else but on Earth, so we use your terms to identify the way you will reach the light. The future, as you are now aware, does not exist. We will be able to share with you many things long-forgotten on Earth, but still here for your use. You will sense peace within you, once you return to the ways of Earth, knowing the world is not the only place. In time, you will see what we mean.

Now we go for a brief respite to gather up the words of our brethren and seek the help of your Guides in directing you into the proper paths to reach the light of God. After you finish reciting the many areas you disagree with us, we suggest you analyze why you do not agree—then you will know where you need to work on *you.*

That is the lesson for this session.

Chapter Eleven

The work of the world is not the work of God! If this is the perception you have, then you must change it. We are here to discuss the real work of God.

The work of God is to integrate each and every soul into the total being that is God—not to send souls to death or destroy your work if you do not achieve the best you are capable of creating. The work of God is not the work of a man or a woman. God is God!

When you were young, you would believe anything you were told. You are no longer young, but many of you continue to believe much that was told to you as a curious child, when you were unable to discern between wisdom and superstitious nonsense. The work of God is not for children to comprehend. It requires a fully-developed intellect, but many people never contemplate God after they pass their childhood years. Obviously, the work of God is not available to children, but the work of God is always there for those developed enough to see and appreciate it.

You are not the only race who has developed to the point where you decide among you that God has no place in your society, but you are the only such race now alive. We are not saying this as an idle warning. If you developed and were never told of the God who is all, you cannot be condemned; but they who neglected to tell you of God's work will be. This is the way of God.

Suddenly the world is noticing the work of Buddha, and even Christ is more active, but neither one is God. They are instruments by which God has reached out to great masses of humans in the past. You are all seeking the second coming of the Messiah, but there is no one coming. A messiah is a person and God is not.

You must find God within you, not outside in the world you have created. In the future of the world, the work of man is not as creative as in the past, because you are not as developed now. If this is obvious to you, you are truly developed; but for most, it is not obvious now.

We are here to help you recognize that God is not as you seek, rather a real presence within each and every one of us. A vast area of unknown exists within You. For example: You never know who You are while on Earth. You know only what is necessary to transcend the evils you create here in order to arrive back at the portal to eternity and go forward.

You do not need to know all your *past lives*. How could you have a *past life* if you never die? We are not being facetious. We are deadly serious. To seek *past life regression* is a waste of time and only serves to satisfy the ego—and the ego receives too much satisfaction!

When the work of your day is done and you are not tired,

you are not going home. You are relaxing and staying in the world. To go home, you must relax, meditate, and seek the inner self. If you never do this, the work of the world will defeat you. When the work of the world defeats you, you are then too tired. You do not see the end result of your work as achieving anything real. This is self-defeating in the truest sense of the words. If you defeat *you*, then the idea of having enemies is not a true concept. You never need enemies. You are all you need to destroy *you*!

Working in the work world of Earth is not the easiest place to be, you say. But where would work be easier? You are here to work; and if you do not work every day, what would help you pass into the next plane?

Certainly idleness is not conducive to spiritual work. It is not the same as relaxation. If you work, you need to relax. If you idle, what do you do for a change of pace? Obviously, you work! That is why the idlers of your society are decadent and evil. They have no real work.

It is the responsibility of each individual to create a job for self to work on all this life. It is not the responsibility of any other person! If you are bitter or stuck, because you believe work of this world should be found for you, then you will return again to this plane. We are concerned because this is a simple concept, yet many Americans cannot grasp it. The rest of the world knows it, but not the most affluent society now. How did this happen?

When the work of the world is not done, the world suffers.

When the work of God is not done, you alone suffer, and suffer, and suffer. It is foolish to follow any leader who does not lead you back to God. If you try to follow an egotistical leader, you are alarmed internally. You can feel the challenge on a very personal level. To ignore this early warning is to place another human above God. You must listen to YOU!

In the early days of Earth, the work of God was so much admired that nothing was done to change it; but in latest times, the Earth is gouged, dug up and moved, and changed constantly. Is this wise? Does this not sound egotistic? Why do you have the power to do this?

You were given dominion over the Earth. It was your responsibility to maintain it, but you are not interested in the life forms always here and now being forced to change, because you are destroying their home as well as your own. This is not to be permitted to continue.

God has issued orders for the future that include the design for the work of man. You will be unable to refuse. The orders of God are not religious. They exist even now, but you are ignorant and refuse to read and understand—let alone pray and meditate in order to hear the works of God explained to you in detail.

Meditation is the foundation of your devotion to God. If you are not meditating and praying, what are you doing? We are aware many try to meditate now and grasp inner peace, because of the turmoil in the outer world, but seldom do you continue once you learn how to block out outer noise. This is a selfish approach to seeking God. You must meditate!

If you are not a meditator, or never contemplate the work of God, you will be unconscious to what is going on in the work of the world. It is now changing. It has to change, if life is to continue on Earth.

No more giant industries polluting the air or contaminating the water! If you continue in these archaic ways of managing people and resources, you will be without air and water before the next generation is deceased and able to reincarnate. This is no idle threat. It is absolutely true!

Ask an astronomer for his prediction on the amount of air left surrounding this planet. He will tell you there is not much. Ask a natural scientist whether we have enough water for all future generations being born and reborn and he will tell you water is not good, nor is there much of it. Think on these things—then make up your own mind.

You have been on Earth for many generations, but for You Earth is only a classroom. It is not the home of souls, nor is it the only work of humans. We see this caught your attention.

You are so simple and easily confused that you do not notice other entities living on Earth, so how would you know you are not always on Earth? If you are not always on Earth— where are you then? Within the solar system, several other planets resemble the consistency of Earth, but none of them are identical to it.

This is not where you run when you are tired of class. You run into the world of the night—or dreams. This is indeed as much a planet as the one you live on now. It does not exist like Earth exists, but it is.

Your minds are full now. Let us go forward. We will return to this another day.

What does the sun do? Did you ever wonder about it? No? Then why is the sun the center of the universe—not Earth? You do not know? Then why are you the only one who is important? That should be easy to answer, but just as unknown to us as to you. We see only frail Earth with aging souls unwilling to leave it. It makes no sense to us, but it does to you.

If the work of God is incomprehensible, why do you think you know everything? We are aware of the need for the other, but we are constantly amazed that you create it. If you did not have negativity, what would you learn on Earth?

We see you now awakening to the real reason you are here on Earth. It is to learn by being challenged how to deal with the power you have. You are challenged in order to build your strength—not to disturb your soul. If you create negative forces, you can destroy them. To ask God to destroy a force which man created is not a serious way to learn.

It is not God's way to interfere—*unless you completely lose the way*. Once God determines this is so, you are taken from the planet and placed on a lower plane. This is not pleasant!

If the source of your negativity is not in heaven, is it on Earth? You are sure you know everything there is to know about Earth, and you say it comes from heaven. That is not true. Negativity is only on Earth. If you learn to control and use it to your advantage, you can move mountains. If you cannot, you are overwhelmed and defeated by its force.

Some people are confused now. We see it is not enough to say negative forces exist. You need examples. We have one.

In this world of your making there are several kinds of people who try to take over the world. They are not leaders, but always strive to contain the world's people and rule them. These people are not wonderful, but you let them take over. If you did know how to control negativity, you could easily control them. If you knew You, you would never listen to them. If you could be *you*—and no one else could be *you*—why believe others could help you be more than you are?

These are serious considerations and questions that must be reviewed by all who are ready to advance. If you and all serious people do not conform to negativity, it is short-lived and does not exist. You will be able to stop anything or anybody who tries to explode or take off with your life. You need to create positive forces to counteract all the negativity currently rampant on Earth.

This situation is not good. You need to achieve balance. Balance is the answer, but you cannot agree on what it is. We see you confusing balance with equilibrium. We refer to the way forces are assigned to different areas of your lives.

You do not seek negativity, but condone it. You do not ask negative people to reach the top of society's ruling classes, but elect them and permit them to be on top. This sort of decision-making enslaves all. You must carefully *re-seek* your own personal goals, then seek people capable of helping you achieve those ends.

What is sought from political figures now is a person who looks good. You want someone who is young, vital, and ignorant of the ways of the world—or so it would appear. If this is the best person to lead, then why do you all cry so loudly for help now? Earth does not need a leader. You as a society believe you do, so it is the decision of you all who should best represent each of you. What is so difficult? Check out their strengths and weaknesses!

Why do you hate anyone who is superior to you? It is the nature of nature to produce superior and inferior beings. It is not natural to prevent the superior from breeding and enlarging the size of society. Your societies today reflect the neglect of this very real consideration. If you are not superior, and the superior are never praised, why should you correct other's shortcomings?

We see you are uncomfortable now. This is then a truth. Whenever you grow uncomfortable, it is true!

In the world of women, a woman who is beautiful, talented,

and able to attract men is hated by jealous women. Why? She personifies what the world says is important. You see? You do! The image the world wants is not necessarily the image you want. You want to be the prettiest, most important, most sought-after female if you are female. If you are male, you do not want such a woman to attain the power she is entitled to by your world's standards.

Jealousy is a terrible, negative emotion that has now reached its highest levels in the history of your world. It is destroying and creating havoc. You need to decide why you fear others. Is it because you are inferior? Is it because you fear they will take away all you have? Do you fear they are better and deserve more than you? Whatever—it is unworthy of a man or woman of God. It is not to be condoned. All must speak out against jealousy, if it is to be beaten back into a controllable size and force now.

When you talk to YOU, ask why you fear. That is the lesson for this session. We need time to regroup, and you need time to rethink all we have said.

Sit still and meditate on ideas that cling to you. Once your mind settles on a single idea, continue to meditate until the next idea comes forward. In time the entire lesson will be yours, and you will then be able to teach it to others.

We go now and seek the sun of our life—God, and his messengers. In the future, angels will come. But for now, we are here.

Chapter Twelve

The work of the Lord of All is never to be judged by man, but every day we hear humans on Earth criticize God. Is this to be allowed? We doubt it.

You are not the only ones who exist on Earth, and your rude manners are not to be condoned. Many of the lessons given are necessary because of the rudeness and crudeness now allowed to permeate every level of your societies on Earth.

If you are so great, why do you seek God? If you have all the answers, why do you think you are in so much trouble now? God directs the work of your hands, but it is your decision whether to use that work for good or evil against other humans.

You are never permitted to do evil against the work of God. That is a presumption of some men and women of *faith* that puzzles us. If God is the creator, who are you to critically judge such work? You who cannot create a pleasant environment for yourself would deem it plausible to criticize God? It is such a ridiculous position to place yourself at any time—but especially now. Now is the time you are unable to be YOU. You are all off-balance.

When the world is over as your classroom, it is over. The

time is coming to remove all who are ready to move to the next plane, but what about those still in the *lower grades?* We do not care to think of them. We are only concerned with those able to understand the meaning of your spiritual truths and act upon them.

If your words are untrue, whose words are truthful to you? The lies of your lips are the lies of all. You are the core and essence of your universe, so if you lie—all lie. No big belief system is required to know this simple fact of life.

If your life is not your life, you seek another. If that life still does not satisfy you, you are *not* able to seek another. You must stand pat and work it out. So many of you have used up your spare life and must now work out this one. If you are incapable of working it out, you are stuck. We advise you to start getting out of your rut now.

Much in the work of God is startling and different from your work and creations. That is due to your limited imaginations. In the work of God, all is possible. In the work of man, only what has been seen can be created. It is so!

We cannot share with you all the ways you differ from others in the universe, but know you are different! Begin to realize this so you can accept the differences you see in other human beings. The differences among people are slight. Your eyes are unable to accept varying shades of color, so how do you expect to accept varying shapes and forms?

When we are gone from Earth, you are to be teachers. We

are here for the sole purpose of helping you get to the next plane. We are not here for any other reason. If that is impossible, we are not condemned, but you are. What if we are right and your ideas of what is to become of *you* are wrong? This is not an easy idea to accept, but it must be absorbed.

We are not in the annals of your time. You have never had a visitation from anyone beyond the realm of angels. We are above that level, but not above angels. God is the supreme ruler of the universal world of us all. We are not above God.

Wherever you are, we are—but we are not here for very long. Your life is eternal, but we are not part of your life. We are here to do the work of God and then return to our work. You will know.

Why we are here is of no importance, if you are unwilling to do what we say. This lesson is about obedience and calling into play all of your past errors of judgment now being held against you. We will help you rectify these errors.

If a human hurts another human or animal maliciously, the dues required to correct this situation are not as easily paid as they would be if you merely harmed them in some superficial way, but you are to pay if you even suspect you are guilty of hurting someone else.

In the full moon of each month is a power that can move tides higher and shake the Earth. At that time, we suggest you present yourself to the heavens and ask God to forgive you. It is not merely a prayer, but a type of humiliation. You are to dress in plain clothes and wear no jewelry or makeup. You are to pray for several hours with your face turned upward toward the moon and ask for forgiveness. If the moon warms your face, it is to be considered a great blessing. If your face is not warmed by the moon then, you must continue to pray and beg for forgiveness for as many full moons to come as is necessary to feel its warmth.

Pagan rituals are not devoid of God. You are! You are full of self and earnestly pursue the good will of your superiors to such an extent that it sickens your soul to be at work or play.

We will never ask you to induce stress or call forth tremendous effort. Simple prayer and meditation will get you out of this world's clutches—not the elaborate rituals and procedures of certain men and women, as well as some churches. This is not the time to begin new religions, either.

So you are called a pagan—so what! Why do you care if others do not favor you? You live. They live. We are not concerned. This is the nature of your reality.

Much of the material channeled in the recent past has concerned itself with negative thought patterns. They are not wrong, but the time to sit and discuss philosophy is over. Now you have to put into action your beliefs. We see many can in theory follow all we say, but when effort is required on your part—no way. This is a serious fault that leads to your own discipline: You will never be freed from Earth.

Why believe, but not pursue it? We are curious. In the works of man is a limited concept repeated over and over. You believe in God, but you do not believe God can help you through the difficulties of your life. You do not ask for help then, you ask after it is over. We often wonder about that.

Why would a woman say with confidence: "I don't have time to learn to meditate, because I'm so deep in trouble and need time to get out of it"? We watched the woman stare into space, but she did not meditate. She could not understand that her work is here and now, and meditation is to be used to aid her in understanding why her work is what it is. Are you like this woman?

If your life is unlike that of others—yet it is not, why do you think others want your work? We often see you hide your thoughts and desires from others and talk only to your Guides about them. We want you to understand it is not necessary to hide your wishes. Instead, wish on the light and love of God and let it go out to the universe. Let everyone hear of it.

Within the hub of the universe is God, and at the furthest reaches of the universe is God. So why are you so sure you are not observed? When you see lights in the heavens, you often say, "Oh, look! There's a flying saucer." What is a flying saucer? Does it have a cup? We are curious and without a clue.

Extraterrestrials (as you call them) are not extra-terrestrial. They live on Earth! You are only now becoming aware others live here, too, but all other planes above yours are fully aware of them, as well as you. That is the primary reason we are here.

Extraterrestrials are here to move and associate with others in their own dimension, as well as in other dimensions. They sometimes get confused and stay too long in your dimension, thus get upset enough that they emit enough energy to reveal their position. You laugh, but you are not at all sure we are wrong.

Now the reason we are here today is not to talk about *extraterrestrials*. We are here now to teach you how to gain favor and access to the next higher plane, so you can leave Earth at the end of this life. You are not to try this if you do not want to be released from Earth then.

With the advent of the *New Age of Aquarius*, all children were informed of it—but not adults. The reason for this was adults formerly could return over and over again, but that is no longer an option. God does not intend to interfere and produce additional clear, running water and pure air, because the last was abused and wasted. This decision is not vindictive. It is the input of all who live on Earth now that caused God to arrive at this decision.

All over people on Earth are crying for help and wish to abandon Earth. All are sorry for the mess created by nuclear attempts to kill off everyone but themselves—whoever they may be—now all are creatively dry. No new solutions have appeared.

No one wants to assume responsibility or lead others out of the war against crime and shame. Whatever you want—you get! It is a simple fact. You do not want to keep Earth whole, nor do you want to be human anymore. So we are here to help you get onto the next plane and away from this work of man that now prevents spiritual growth.

Women are leaders of the home, and men are leaders of the world. Both areas are equally important, but women suddenly became jealous of men and wanted what they had. This is the critical change anticipated, but it is unnecessary to give up this world as a classroom in which negative thinking can be overcome by positive work. Women will be leaders, if they assume the work of The Holy Spirit. If they do not, who will do it?

When women are at war, it is a vicious time. Men are used to war and games, but women hate to war and play games. Therefore, the war of today in your world is vicious, mean, and not to be continued. The war of today creates an ugly world for tomorrow. All involved in war games must stop! They know who they are.

In the center of each life is God, and it is impossible to push God into a corner. You are the end of God's line. No further beings have been created.

It is your work to raise all the worlds of yesterday on Earth and create a unified sequence of events in order to qualify for graduation from this plane. If your lives are unequal to the best of others' lives, how can you be sure you will be advanced? Wherever you are, God seeks YOU. It is not hocus-pocus. It just is!

We see you squirm. You fear God—and you should. God is not You or your playmates on Earth, but the supreme judge of all.

In the work you do and play you permit, you display all the

ways you are *you*. If you cheat, carry tales, and act vicious, all are aware of your conceit and fear of no man, but they will all see you go to Hell.

Hell is this classroom on Earth. It does not exist anywhere else. Your return to Earth is the same as being sent to *Hell*. Heaven is being able to move to a higher plane, if you so desire.

Some return to help The Guides, but few actually do. Sometimes you even go astray then, which is what happened in recent times. As a way of punishment, they have to answer for their lives all over again. No one will be spared—not even angels who reside on Earth. Oh, yes, we may not have told you—only inferred—but angels dwell on Earth. You may be one yourself.

Angels are unaware they are angels. If they have not kept meditative contact with the higher planes, they are unaware of their purpose on Earth. Angels are here to enable the change-over at the end. They are like military police. We mean no disrespect, but angels are warriors of God.

When this world is over and you are fully exonerated or honored for your part in making the best of a life continually beset with problems and negativity, we will certainly be aware of your success or failure. You are our pupils. We as teachers— like teachers everywhere, are correctly made responsible for our pupils' success and failure. We are not afraid. We are sure you will be able to rise to the next plane.

This is the end of this session, but not the end of our lessons.

We are not yet to the real meat of this work. It takes time to prepare *you*. We will continue to do so—then we will deliver all you need to know.

Chapter Thirteen

This is the time of the world changing into the work of God instead of man. This is the time of the world's release of its captive energies that will force man to fall back to ancient beliefs and efforts to appease God in order to survive. This is the time of the world's work being destroyed in order to let God live on Earth. You will know.

Never be afraid of this time. It is the time of change and the time of growth. You fear change and growth, yet nothing in your life is comfortable now. You will be glad to see the changes!

When you are *you*, and you are going to be *you* soon, the work of God is an ideal you will zealously pursue and want others to follow you. This is not to say they will. They are not the only ones to begin doubting the fullness of these times. You are not the only ones to begin to see the light. We are here to help all of you.

In the next century of your time, we will be actively pursuing the ends of the Earth. In this century (*Ed. Note: This book was channeled in 1993*) we fully pursue the populous areas with much effort in order to secure the greatest number of converts from the old ways to the ways of God. You will see vast numbers of people reel from the effects of this. You will know you are not alone.

In the beginning of these times we could not seek a place in your classrooms on Earth. We were not ready to work with you. We had to learn to use your energy and minds, which was difficult for all of us.

We have learned much by channeling through some women and men, but the effort to reach you is too much for their frail voices and bodies. We see it now. We will stretch our goals over a longer period of time and will not increase the use of channels. This is not to say we will not channel, but rather we are not as likely to do so from now to the end.

If you feel the need to say something, then say it; but do not say we are channeling through you, as many did in the past. This is not caused by a need to express hatred of evil done in the world, but fear that evil will be delivered to that individual if she or he announced it was their deep conviction and opinion. Your world does not now honor people with deep convictions and opinions about God's will, but soon they will be so much in demand it will not be necessary to claim to channel another plane's entity.

Within the world of your time is a fear of all who look like a different species or possess rare features, but in the near-term all of you will see rarities abound and growing, and you will not see them as ugly. You will recognize their innate qualities and abilities for the first time. This is absolutely necessary if you are to be enlightened and able to move off this Earth plane.

When a group of individuals decides to create their own little world—and do so, you become convinced they are evil. This was never the case in the past, but it is today. Why? If you are so sure they are evil, it appears to us you harbor evil thoughts within you and fear they also harbor them within. That is your problem—not theirs. We do not condone exclusive cliques, but sets of people often work better than large unmanageable crowds of fanatics and idealists. Let them work for you. Do not fear!

Whether or not you personally can carry forth the banner of God is not the worry of our panel of teachers, we are here to seek out those who could do it. If you can, then continue and develop your self. If you cannot—and we know some of you cannot, let the rest go—do not pursue them as heretics or use such other mean-intentioned epitaphs to color their work for God. *Epitaph is the word we want. The Scribe suggests another word, but we know what we want.*

If your life is so deep into debt that you despair for your sanity, why do you think tomorrow will be better? Why would you buy on credit what you cannot pay for today? The wave of despair hitting your world is due to this inability to pay for what has always been paid for in advance by previous generations.

You have had your fun, but now you figure out ways to get out of paying for it. This dishonesty is the root of your character and explodes into the framework of your entire society. You will reap what you have personally sown, and society is reflective of your character.

If all were honest, which is obviously untrue at this time in your development, your lives would be serene and comfortable in the work you do and with the people who fill your lives. In the world around you and above you are people who do not like this lack of trust; they always pay their own way. They will be the leaders of the future, not those in debt.

Debt reflects how you value *you*. It also reflects your ideals. If you are unable to hold down a job for long, or refuse to do so, we are aware your society looks askance at you; but if you overspend your purse and live deep in debt, no one sees anything wrong in that. This is the edge of the world you live in, but not the core. The central theme of life on Earth is balance. If you are over the edge in debt, you are over the edge!

Why go into debt? We often ask why, but always know. We ask in order to see what your thought processes will produce. When you go into debt, you obviously do it to impress others!

If you need something, God provides enough. If you want something, God will provide it—provided it is not detrimental to You. With that knowledge you should never need to go into debt. If you do, then pay it off as soon as possible. Never borrow to impress another—only to pay off bad credit or people who have extended services to you in good faith.

When another person extends credit to you, it is because they trust you. If you do not pay it back, *karma* is attached to it. If you let them trust you, you are responsible—never the lender— for the results of not paying the bill. You cannot blame banks, insurance companies, or usurious individuals. It was always you who went to them, not the other way around; therefore, you pay back or are condemned for not keeping your word.

To declare bankruptcy is an admission of your inability to manage, but divorcing a mate is no such admission. To divorce another person, as long as it does not harm children of the mating, is of no consequence to God or us. You see, families are your world's way of handling the propagation of your species, but not our way. These legal proceedings have been created in the past to secure the future of the race. One reason why we are not appalled at the lack of commitment in your marriages now is that you will not be able to add many more souls to the world you live in now.

The diminishing of marriage as a ritual is not to say people will not continue to love and seek to be together. You need one another. You do not do well alone. Your lives are an intricate network of reasoning and belief in yourselves above God.

If you are alone, you begin to fear all who live on Earth, but seldom resort to believing in God. This then creates individuals who wreck havoc on others at will. These malcontents range all over the world seeking trouble and harming others, but they seldom are seen for who they are. You are not to be deceived by them. Shoot them down in the streets if they shoot your innocents down in the streets. We have no trouble with that at all. It only makes sense to destroy anyone or anything that hurts the welfare of the majority of your people. They are responsible for their own deaths. You are letting them end their lives sooner.

Capital punishment is never evil, if the state decides it is necessary to rid the world you live in of a person who is anti-social. Anti-socialism is a mortal sin. It will prevent you from entering the next plane. You must always live together on Earth as brothers and sisters. If you do not, you die and come back again to try it all over again. If you are executed, you die and come back again to try all over again, but you have been absolved of the guilt of the previous life. If you escape punishment, you will be required to make recompense for it in the next life or two.

We are here to advance you—not to hold up the line. We want you to be able to advance; and if that means execution, then so be it. You are in full control of your life always. If you decide to harm another person, you will be made to repay for any damage—one way or another, and it is better to repay while on Earth than to wait until you are judged and moved to the other side.

When you are judged at the end of this life, you are not asked why you did something. You are told you did something that harmed another and asked how you wish to repay, then you decide.

If you elect to repay in one lifetime for what evil you did to others in the previous life or two, you may elect to take on such onerous burdens so no one can ever say you did not fully repent your sin. You may decide to have a hideous illness befall you at the best time in your life or decide to die quite young. These are ways some choose to show God reverence when they are unable to pay back the individual soul they previously harmed.

Some will leap to the conclusion that all people who have hideous illnesses or die young are paying back for evil they have done, but you would be entirely wrong to do so. That is ego talking—not God.

You can reclaim a lost life, but you can also decide to end your quest for knowledge on Earth by taking on a double assignment. A double assignment is best described as one where the individual is born with an incurable disease and unable to be the person he or she once was. This *handicap* is given if you were so exalted in spirit at the time you elected to incarnate or reincarnate to the Earth plane and wished to develop certain aspects of your multi-faceted personality and soul.

When ready to die (as you like to say), we will be able to explain anything you care to ask about the process, but we do not deliver long speeches. We tell you only what you need to know. This information is delivered in such short bursts of energy that you do not know you got it until you are dead to this world.

People who often refer to their experience at the time of traumatic ending of one cycle of life and the retooling for another cycle as a *near death experience* are unable to express what they were told. It was in another system and in another frame of reference, but it was said. They are not exaggerating the experience, but they are not to be held in awe, either.

You are just as experienced when you enter another episode of life more slowly and decide to renew your faith in God, Christ, Buddha, Allah, or whatever faith you have chosen to follow on Earth. You are *reborn* regardless of whether or not it came in one cataclysmic scene or over a period of months or years. This is your decision.

It is also your decision to renege on God's plans for *you* on Earth. That is why you are never to blame God. You have full power to choose every day you live on Earth, and you are responsible for all your choices or lack of success.

When deep down you feel you are not being true to you, it is the despair of your entire soul—not just your Earth-bound personality. Whenever you get off track and cannot get back into the traces of what you are here to do on Earth, you will experience a withdrawal of energy by your soul's Guides. You will be unable to pursue with vigor the course(s) you choose, but still able to do whatever you want to do. God does not permit your Guides to interfere. You are able at any time to seek guidance from them, but they may not take control of your life—even for a short time.

You will now see time is of the essence in all of your daily work, because the time warp you prepared for this age is now beginning to speed up. Time to manifest a belief is no longer approximately six months to two years. In the near future such time will shrink to three months to one year—cutting it in half. Some of you do not yet realize you create everything in your life. It will be truly amazing to see your reluctance in the future to think evil, once you see how quickly it comes back to you.

If you need lessons on reality, we know of many who have begun work in your plane with teachers of our plane. Seek them out through their work. Do not honor anyone merely because they can channel. Honor only their work. If all they do is channel, then God will reward them for their efforts. If they channel and work hard for God, man will reward them also. You need not honor anyone who does not live by the words they channel. They will be paid enough for their work.

Work is not the same for all of us. We each seek different goals. We are not alike in any way. We think and believe differently. We will never be the same.

So why do you strive to be alike while on Earth? In the work of Earth and your world, you are secretly yearning to be accepted by all men. Why? If men are not the epitome of God's work, why would you limit yourself that way?

We are not afraid of you, but too many of you are afraid of us. This is because you do not see us. Why else do you seek out psychics who have clairvoyant ability? You have clairvoyant ability, too, but may not choose to develop it. Is it because you lack ambition, are too lazy to meditate and visualize long enough, or are you superstitious like unlearned peoples of the rural back roads of the world? You decide that for yourself.

If you wish to develop *psychic abilities*, a term your society created to mean many different things, we cannot help you. You have to go within your own mind and seek out the wisdom that is there. Your Guides can help you, but may choose not to do so. If you have abused such abilities (not powers) in the past, you may be permitted to develop them only after a long period of refitting and retooling your previous lives' abilities, so they will serve God—not you or other people now.

In life, as you know it, all have been blessed with at least one particular skill or ability from the psychic realm. It can be used to help you all through life, but it is always your decision to do so. We are not here to help you psychically develop or gain access to your inner wisdom. We are much more direct in our approach, because we do not have the luxury of time to develop and nurture you. We need your cooperation now—not ten or twenty years from now.

If you read this book many years after it is first published, and we hope that is a possibility, you will see none of this is too dramatic. You then may be angry because we were not firmer in our resolve, but we are teachers—not dictators or visionaries.

We can now see this lesson has been going on for a very long time and our Scribe is not as into her own work now as she is on vacation. We will not overstay our time, since it does drain her somewhat.

If you need help, ask your Guides to read to you or direct you to material or people who can help you right now to understand any area of this book that confuses you. You will not be without enlightenment soon. Your Guides can speak to you in many different ways. They are not restricted to speaking and writing. They may send others to you or present your requests by way of another's writing or speaking.

We will be gone now, but will return.

Chapter Fourteen

The way of your work is not the way of this work. We do not fully comprehend the handicap you have of being unable to think and then achieve it easily. It is difficult for us to visualize and think on something without creating it immediately. This is a great problem for all of you.

In the work of your plane, all you do is of the most importance to *you*. In the work of our plane we are not important. God is all, and we are not the work of God. You think you are works of God, but you are merely created by God—not the work of God. There is a difference!

When you seek out the help of other people, usually it is only to help you. You do not seek out the help of other people and then go and help other people. That is the way of God— and you are not that way. Some humans seek out others to help others, but they always seek credit for doing so. They do not do it without a reason. This is the way of man.

When you seek God, you seek God to help you. You do not seek God to assist in work that must be done on Earth to help others. The work of God is not your work, but you think it is. If God creates, then leaves the creation to achieve its goals, how do you think God will assist you in being better than other creations?

Why you are here on Earth is now of little interest. The important thing is for you to leave Earth. You must leave. It is only a matter of time until it is of no further use to you as a human being. Once the air is exhausted and water does not run clear, you are unable to live. Therefore, we are here to help you escape.

God has given you the sense to be able to compute and figure out solutions, but it is your job to use those skills. If you are not willing to spend time and effort now, you will die. It is not a difficult decision. It is simply the only solution.

Once the work of God is destroyed, God is not of any further use to you. We see you do not understand. We mean once God cannot use you, you are no longer of use. Does that explain it well enough? No, you do not understand. We will explain it as a story.

If you are unable to understand something, ask for help. If the teacher you ask does not know—and it is not always possible for a teacher to know—you think the teacher failed you, but the teacher did not. You are who has to find the answer—not the teacher. If the teacher asks a question and you cannot answer it, it is the teacher's problem—not yours.

If you are given work to do and do not do it, your life is not over until it is done—and that can take many lifetimes. We suggest you do your old work first, then look to the problems of this life. Once the old work is done, you are free to be you and achieve all you are meant to be in this life; but if you neglect the old work and strive only to achieve the new assignment, you will not be free at the end of this life to pass beyond and go onto the next plane.

The work of your world is not the work of any other plane. It is the work of humans and requires certain things not present anywhere else in the universe. You must accomplish these tasks or be confined to this planet. If you dare to stay for another lifetime, you may not be able to escape. That life may have been placed in the line of destruction of the planet. To be sure, get off Earth this time!

To get off Earth this time, you need only acquire a little bit of life. You do not need a lot of living to be free of it. It is often thought you need to experience every facet of human life in order to pass to the next plane, but that is a fallacy bred by those who enjoy life on Earth and have no desire to grow to the next level of spiritual development. Yes, there are many who come back life-after-life so they may exist on Earth and accumulate many experiences, but that is not the order of things. The order of God's work is to experience life on a material plane, succeed, and then move to a higher plane.

When you are through with this world, we will help you accelerate your growth in order to make up for lingering too long here. It is often seen that you lose your way here, but we never fully realized how difficult it is to live here. For that reason, we will help you all.

Whatever you do, do not let anyone else work for you in

an attempt to deliver your soul to God. We see many pay someone to be *you*. Yes, we know you do. We have seen people hire others to take charge of their jobs, their families, and their homes. They do nothing for themselves—even think God is on the way to being their employee, too. This is not at all funny. God is not amused. You do not hire people to worship, but you do hire people to take care of your spiritual needs.

When you hire another to care for your children, do you inspect them to discover how they were raised? Are you careful about their mannerisms and behavior patterns to insure your children are not copying the wrong behavior of people who are inferior in many ways to you, rather than copying your ways? We see you do not check enough.

When you hire a consultant to take your job and do it better, do you really know if they can do it? We know you trust them. You do not want to learn to do the work, so you trust anyone rather than do it. You also do that with spiritual matters. We watch you seek gurus and teachers who do not live by the standards we teach, nor are they acceptable to God, but you trust them to clear the way for you. No one can do that for you.

You must worship, study, and meditate. If you wait until you are old or perhaps not as busy, we will not avail ourselves to you then. We are only here now. You are here until you can leave. That is your problem—not ours.

In your world today, males are not as likely to hire men to do their work as females are, but in the past men often hired women to be objects of sexuality and desperately fought to keep women down. Today, men do not get such luxuries easily. They have to amass much money before women will sell themselves to them, but it is still done. It will always be so. It is the way of your world. This type of slavery is not unwholesome, if the individuals are not working to free their souls, but it does prevent them from working out of this plane. So, we are now against such divisions of favors. We wish to see such practices stopped so each individual can progress rapidly to the next plane.

When you are unable to be *you*, which is the case for most of your life, we see you become upset and disturbed. You envy those who are true to themselves. You seek to destroy them. You hate their ways and work against them. This is no threat to them, but this is a definite threat to your life. If you do not harness your energies and make them flow in positive directions, you cannot overcome jealousy and hatred. These are two of the most prevalent waves of destruction threatening life on Earth.

Jealousy is more prevalent among women and hatred among men, but both are killers. You need only see yourselves from this distance to know all suffer from the effects of it daily. We cry out at times over the evil done due to your being jealous of another for something you also possess, but are unwilling to develop. This is the shame of humans. Laziness is the root of much jealousy and is now a sin of far greater depth than man is aware of today. Soon you will notice we are not wrong in naming it as the third killer of emotional health.

You must work hard every day! It is the only way to avoid being confined to Earth for another lifetime. In the work of your hands you cannot see its beauty as well as others can, but you see the beauty of others' work. This can be twisted into jealousy and envy—which can destroy all you have. You must weed jealousy out of your soul before you can grow and prosper.

The world has much to recommend it to all souls, but you cannot see all it has to offer, because you yearn for what we have. We do not yearn for what you have, because we know you do not appreciate anything. That is the real basis of envy. You do not realize you (each and every one) possess something of value others do not have, and you do not seek to know what it is. If you know, you do not do enough work to prosper.

If you direct your efforts to locate the gold mine within you, and dig deep and fully reinforce the deepest tunnels, you will be able to mine your mind and body all your life and never want for anything. That is God's way. But if you reflect upon the gifts of others and never seek to find your own, you will never be in the same position. You give them the advantage—not God.

Whatever you desire is here, but you desire everything at one time. You are greedy like the hungry lamb. You cannot drink it all, but you want to drink everything in sight. Learn to slow your impulses and urges and control them so you can have all you need. When you learn how to do this, you are free of the temptations of this world. No one hurries after what can readily be obtained.

Whether or not you can live on Earth successfully is not a concern of ours. We are not your Guides. We are teachers who are here to accelerate the pace at which humans learn their lessons and graduate from this plane. We will not work on you individually—that is the work of your Guides. We will not work for you as a group—that is the work of High Guides or Master Guides. We are not here to create a class. We are here to tutor you in the ways of ascending to the next plateau where you will be able to gather strength enough to help you move toward the light of God.

Your life on Earth is not as difficult as life on lower planes, so some believe this is heaven, but it is not heaven (believe us). You are not in heaven while on Earth. You are in *Hell*, and if you are not permitted to ascend to the next plane (you refer to it as going to heaven), you will return to *Hell* or Earth. It is always your decision!

If you want to move up, you work hard every day and get along with every man, woman, and child you meet—and never sin against anyone. If you prefer to lag behind and seek out further experiences on this plane, you do exactly what you want. We cannot know if you understand or not. We only see the results of your life.

We do not listen to the defense garnered by You and your Guides before the High Guides at the end of each life, but we know *you*. We can see *you*. We are aware of your needs and desires, yet you know nothing about us.

How do you think we can teach you if we are unable to know

your weaknesses? No one can teach who does not first know the student. Once the student is ready to learn, the teacher need only see the level of his or her advancement to know the student. It does not take more than that. Personal involvement with students does not help teachers, but it improves learning for some students. You are not to be personally involved with us, so this aid is unavailable to you now.

When the world is not awake, but you are, you fear many things. When the world is awake and you are awake, you can fully develop. We are here to awaken the world, and you are here to fully develop. Together we are a team of great value to God. God is the captain of our team and not worried about the final score—only how we are doing individually. We are here to help you improve yourself—not the score.

We are not of the same world as *you,* and we are not interested in attending to your work. We are more interested in knowing you as a race. We see so many distinct ways to work out problems that we often wonder how you can be considered a race. You are so slow in coming to conclusions, yet so quick to demand payment. If you are in a race, how do you know who is winning? We see no finish line.

You have devised many ways of developing your expertise in the *workplace,* but none of these ways is satisfactory when it comes to rewarding the winners. You often change rules halfway through the game so someone other than the winner wins. This is done out of malice and spite more often than due to realizing the game does not matter—only what it does for the entrants.

You will not admit it, but you do not like winners! When you spot winners, you immediately set out to undo them. You sort through rules and ways of action that let you work evil against the winner, without being caught doing it. That is the real evil of the workplace.

The workplace is not to be allowed to continue now. It has produced too many evils. It is not a place of spiritual development and growth, and will not be allowed to harm more people. In the future all who have gained from the distribution of wealth as a result of cheating will be forced to share it with all who were robbed or cheated of their fair share. You will see much of this now. We see it beginning to take effect in other areas—not just America, Europe, and Asia. The last will definitely be first. You will never again seek to stay on Earth.

≫

The text for today is:
You are not alone!

You are always watched. You are never sought out for any particular reason, but viewed by many who are adept at measuring behavior against cause and effect. You will know of it when you advance, but for now—take heed.

When you first come to Earth you are asked to live with a family or person unknown to you at that time, but may be related to you over a vast period of time. You never know while on Earth who you were before you came here, but you may have memories of other times.

We do not condone the remembering of many lifetimes solely for the benefit of ego expansion. You are not to sit down and try to review all your *past lives*. You do not have *past lives*, because you never die! You are eternal and will always be eternal, but if you prefer this term, we will accept it.

If you lived before, why are you here now? You are here to be *you!* No one else is to be You. We are not You, nor are *you* one of us.

We seek nothing from You. You are to use us if you need us. We cannot offer you our knowledge—you must seek it. We will be gone before you can be helped, if you hesitate to seek knowledge from us now, because we are not long on Earth. It is your decision.

We go now to another place on Earth so we may review and report what *we* find to *our* teachers. You see—only God is above all. When we are ready, we will again anger some of you as we enlighten many more.

We will be back after the break of time you call a day; however, we do not recognize it as a day. Your variety of time is not like what exists anywhere else in the universe. Your time is only of use to you. For us, it is a curiosity and hindrance. When we are prepared to teach, you are asleep. When The Scribe is unable to write, we have to wait for the *proper time*. It is a nuisance, but we are prepared to make such complications mere inconveniences.

We will seek out others who know of your ways and wiles

to help define the life you need to seek, and then we will arrive at a conclusion. Never conclude anything without first arriving at a conclusion; however, today's conclusion is not a conclusion. We are merely breaking for a short time for rest and activities the Scribe needs in order to live. We will be back more quickly than in the past.

Chapter Fifteen

This is the time to begin a new life
—not today, but NOW!

〰

In the world you live there are people unwilling to let the life of you and your kind exist. They want you to believe as they do. They will ridicule and deride you for being devout and not swayed by their brand of religious conviction. It is up to you to change them! We do not care to involve ourselves, but if you do, we will send angels.

When you are the only one who believes as you do, it is not hard to devote yourself to God; but if you are not the only one, it becomes hard to avoid distractions from others who are adamant in their beliefs and sure you do not fully understand or you would believe as they do. We are here to avoid such confusion. We will help strengthen your convictions and erase many of the small fissures developing which may connect and cause a major faction to break away. God is not for a special segment of the population and against the rest. That is always ego talking!

This life is not the only life you have. You are a multi-faceted being who must go through many phases before you arrive at

God. This is not the first plane you have lived on, but try to make sure this is the last time you live on this one. If you linger, we are sure you will not have enough to live on. You need too much to be capable of living in the next century. If you had been less inward and more outward in your planning, the world would not be so restricted in the near future, but we digress.

In the near future you will be the only one who can help *you*. We will be gone, and all The Guides will be busy preparing work for the next phase of those *graduating* from Earth. You do have your own Guides, but The Guides so active now are not as singular as your Guides. These Guides often oversee the lives of several people on Earth in order to make sure they do not consciously harm anyone else as they achieve their personal goals. Guides of entities are their souls in a different form and shape, but *The Guides* we refer to here are not like them. These Guides are majestic, so you may not seek them. They seek you—like archangels might.

Even if you do not use the term *Guide*, it is still the same. We suggest you consciously refer to them as Guides and High Guides, because it reminds you that you are in charge on this plane and they only provide guidance. You must make all decisions and do all the work! We are not going to use a different term, but you may if it suits you—but remember the difference.

Presently, individual Guides are referred to as Higher Self and Super Conscious and other such terms, but the term *Guide* is to be the one used. We will identify the Guides as individual, or if they preside over individual Guides, as High

Guides. This simplification can be used as an example, but is not quite accurate. You will know when you move into the higher planes.

When the work of The Guides is done and you cannot be *you*, we will send angels. The work of The Guides is now. The world is to be free of the great anger and terrible wars between you and your fellow humans. But if it still rages by the time Earth depletes its last oxygen and water, angels will immerse their swords of light and enter your work and rid the Earth of doubters and deceivers. Angels are not Guides, but warriors of God. You now see angels, but in those times you will not. Angels are messengers now, but not then.

As the work of God enlarges on Earth to encompass the world you live in, as well as the world of other entities sharing this same planet, we will help you live as one. Teachers are needed whenever the world changes, but it is the warriors who make it actually happen. Not one of you will easily change how you think, thus some have to be forced to see God. That is not the best way, but it is the only way for those blinded by ignorance or ego to the will of God.

Your life is your life, but it is not your life to waste. It was created by God and given as a gift to *you*. If you care not for the gift and waste it, you will not be given such a precious gift again. You will have to earn it the next time. To earn such a gift, you must not think you are a god or goddess. This line of prayer—or is it play—is mocking Almighty God. You will not live if you do not honor the sacredness of The Holy Spirit and God.

The Holy Spirit is a term you use, but do not understand. We use it differently than how you use it. We see The Holy Spirit, but you do not. When The Holy Spirit descends upon you, you feel it—but it is not an emotion. It is the actual sense of God's Spirit in action—not the sense of action. We will know the Spirit of God is here when Earth can no longer spin.

Why must you live on and on and on in this plane when the next plane is so much more desirable? The next plane is ultimately the next step in your evolution, but so many have stayed too long on Earth because Earth appears to them to be the end. We argue now over why this is. We cannot agree. We seek answers.

You must seek and tell us why you cling to Earth when you are supposed to seek God. We will hear you. We will listen and harbor no grudge if you are unable to define why you wish to live and reincarnate again and again to Earth.

When the work of God is done on Earth, you will know it when told. The world you built will be destroyed and eradicated from your memory. It would serve no purpose to remember kindergarten or first grade procedures once you move to higher levels of education. You cannot accurately remember such events, so it is foolish to cling to them. We often hear you remember events from your youth as though they were lived only a short moment ago. This puzzles us, but is perhaps partly to blame for your belief in life on Earth being the best of all possible worlds. *Remember: A child cannot measure life.*

We are here today to talk about the work of God and man,

but you are unable to submit to such talk unless a worldly person who knows of God. If you have never been involved in the world, you will be unable to pass the test at the end of this life. If you are not aware of God, you automatically fail. So it is significantly important that you do not let us waste time on simple ideas, rather let us work on the complex issues you need to know in order to fully advance at the end of this life.

In the work of God you will see many things that are of no use to you, but you never see anything of no use to anyone. The work of God is for all. You do not necessarily need the outcome of the working parts of a machine, but someone else must need it or it would not have been invented.

Machines are not of God. Mankind produces machines for the use of all, but trees, flowers, and animals were created and placed at your disposal. You have never been able to genetically create a living thing from nothing. You can isolate cells needed for creation and growth, then cultivate and nurture them, but you are never given the ability to create. God is your creator.

When an artist paints or sculpts, the work is said to be the creation of the artist, which is not entirely true. The work is the result of divine inspiration. You must let your artistic abilities develop. If you treat them badly or ignore them, you will suffer from a lack of strength in the area where God is most likely to appear. If your life is full of strange and wonderful things, you most likely are an artist of some type.

Rejoice in the ways of God, since art is the output of your happiness. When an artist is not creating, the artist is unhappy. But if the artist thinks about creating, the Spirit of God descends and moves and creates the final impression of the work, thus the artist is inspired. Such a day is remembered.

Think back to when you were divinely inspired to create. Was it yesterday? Was it long ago? You must not let too many days go by before you create art. If you do, your life is diminished to such a great extent that it feels stifling and boring to be alive. You will not fear life if you work and create ideas God fully developed and stored in your mind.

What is the difference between an artist and a musician? There is no difference. You are all creative geniuses who may be free of the boundaries of Earth any time you wish. It is your life—not the life of an artist or musician. You create your life and God is the sole provider of the material. You do not give life, yet you live.

In the end, Earth is not of great importance to you. Now it is the only world you know, but it is not the only world. You will be out of this plane only a short time when you realize who has power and the worth of that power. When you fully recognize you have no power compared to other more highly-evolved souls, you will seek knowledge.

In the schools of Earth, no one seeks knowledge now. All seek power, which is how ridiculous beings are made to appear wise. You will not remember such abuses once you arrive on the other side; nevertheless, you have been harmed by lack of instruction. Long ago instructors were sent to help you use works of God placed here for your lifelong pursuit of God's ways, but you cannot remember any lessons—that is why we are here.

When you see the end in sight, all will want to be ready. Why wait? In the beginning all were ready to learn all there was to know about Earth and themselves, but not anymore. This is a terrible waste of time.

Time on Earth is your time, but elsewhere time as a concept is not of your devising. It is the schedule and scorecard that helps us know when and how we need to advance in order to achieve the goals necessary to merge our souls with God. It is never to be wasted.

Why are you so often tired? We see The Scribe is tired. She is not as into the work of our minds this day. She has not had as much rest between sessions, but it is the only way to pursue this work. She will be rested when we return, but all of life on Earth appears to lack energy now. It often affects your moods and judgment.

We see you fight often and not well, because you do not sleep enough. Correct that first. It is an easy lesson.

We are unable to continue to talk at a great rate, but will try to get one last idea over to you before we leave. You will not be the only ones hurt if you do not prepare to leave at the end of this life. You will be one of several types of beings unable to continue to live on Earth.

The air is necessarily thin and stagnant, because of the work of others who are clear and worthy of God. In most cases your work is neither clear nor dedicated to God; you are destroyers of their world. We seek them when not addressing you. If you wish, we will seek to know ways you can be of assistance to us in helping others also flee Earth. However, this is not the lesson.

Today, you will see the winter of the soul about to begin. It is not the best time to plant seeds, but we must. If you could do one thing to insure your placement on the next plane, would you do it? We know many will say 'Yes'. However, few will do it. We will teach you anyway.

In this world there are several ways to be. You may help others or not. Another way of stating that fact: You may be of service or disservice. You may not be of worth to anyone or you may have great responsibility. These are types of choices you have made. In the end we make choices for you—tasks you must complete or not. You will be given no choice then—and we will grade you harshly.

The work of man is not difficult; however, you do not like to work. These are the words of too many now. You work, but all around you others sit and plot and scheme and devise ways to avoid all responsibility. You complain you work too hard to make up for their lack of cooperation, but they will not be answering for *you* at the end. You will not be spared if you do not work because others did not work. You are not to be spared if you did nothing to help because it was not the fashion or the mores in your countries now. We will never listen to such alibis and lies. You will not be believed!

In the work of your hands is the work of God. We will help you capture the essence of hard work. It is up to you to follow through and do it. We are not your slaves, nor are angels here to do your bidding. You must never seek an angel to do your work. It will not be condoned. Your life is to be of service to mankind, and angels are not servants of man.

You will suffer if you do not obey! Enough warning—your life is yours to live and destroy, but you have now been taught. You may never use that excuse again.

We now go to the end of days here on Earth—which you fear much. We do not wish to worry you. We wish to get you moving and working on your lessons now. If you cannot do them, call us while we are here. Maybe we will answer. We seldom tutor, but there is a chance we may not be busy when you call.

Chapter Sixteen

The work of the world is not done, but the work of *you* and your soul *is* done. You need not linger here long. It does nothing to enhance *you*. It is of no great value to be here long after the last of your lessons have been learned. We see you long to stay to the bitter end—but why? You are not the only one to be awakened at this time, but you are the only one who counts to YOU.

We are unafraid of what you desire, but what you do not want concerns us. We see you do not know of God and all the many miracles performed daily around you. You have been blind all your life. You see only the surface of life—not into the depths and passions of others. Likewise they, too, do not see *you*. What you need is intensity of love and passion in all you do, but you settle for far less.

Wherever *you* are, we or You are not far from the center of your universe. Until the end, You are the only one who can save *you*. Neither we, nor your Guides, nor angels, nor any other entities can save you. Only *you* can be You! If you choose to ignore and disclaim this responsibility, you die—only to come back around again.

This is why we are here. We do not want you to come back

again to redo what you can do right now. Perhaps we care more than you that *you* are saved?

Some people ask, "Are you saved?" We do not. We are here only to share with you the knowledge of those who have gone before you and hope to see you soon on the upper planes. We seek not survivors or death for anyone who does not care. We are here only to teach.

Your life is to be the complete creation of *you*. It is not the work of anyone else. If it were, you would not be held responsible. Since it is totally your work and your responsibility, you cannot weasel out of it at the end. It is the only work you have that is meaningful. It is the only work that will survive.

You are not dead. You live. You can be exactly who you wish and strive to be. It does not matter where or why you choose to be where you are right now. It is your decision, so do not ask for release from your obligations.

When an adult brings another soul to life, it is that adult's responsibility for that lifetime to make sure the offspring is never without instruction and help, but it is not necessary to support that child once he or she leaves home after achieving maturity, or *adolescence*, as you call it.

Sub-adults are now wrecking peace and harmony like no one has ever done before, and it is the fault entirely of adults. No child has the ability to take control. Control is not what they want. They want to be respected and appreciated for themselves, just as you do. If they are denied basic training and instruction in the ways of your people, they will be crushed and defeated by society.

Your laws are too strict now to enable anyone to be free, and these laws do not work. They are so difficult to understand that you need special people to interpret them. This leads to a state of chaos and confusion among the rank-and-file of the population that will not end until laws are reformed and made easy to comprehend and follow by common people—which includes you.

When a child grows into a man or woman, the resulting individual is responsible for their life and may never blame those who reared or taught them. We purposely used plural, because each of you are many people in one. You are not singular in your mores or purposes as an individual.

Your society is complex, but not as difficult to understand as you perceive it to be. Work on *you* and the world is not difficult to understand or navigate through its many levels of socialization. You are made up of many different and difficult personality traits; but if you understand *you*, you understand the world.

We see you do not think much of yourself or you would not doubt everyone else. We are here to help you see yourself as a God-like individual who is capable of greatness. Gratitude is the basis of all greatness. You forget to thank God, your parents, your country, your own being for all you have, instead take such things for granted.

We will not let you continue to ignore the work of others who help you. You will now be instructed to seek out all who helped you, in order to help them continue to help others. The way they reached you worked, so it is a good method.

Consider all of the people you know. Who is the most important person to you? Who was always with you? Who tried—even if they could not reach you? Who cares about you? When your list is complete you will have the means to begin your next lesson. We will help you achieve the exact degree of identity you desire, but you must work, too. If you do not recognize anyone as helping you, we are unable to help you— because you are a fool!

Much of life is spent in a laboratory experimenting with the life force and how it can spread to enable you to live on many different wavelengths, but little is spent on *you*. You seldom seek knowledge of the universe to develop yourself. If you do, you are often ridiculed into dropping the search. That is not the fault of others, but the sole fault of *you*.

You are not here to impress the world. You are here to leave nothing undone that needs to be completed in order for you to progress to the next plane. If you are concerned only about the reactions of other people, your plans and place in life are neglected. We do not give out grades, but you will certainly fail at the end if you do not accomplish your life's goals!

You do not get advanced certification for being good to others, but it helps if the final score is close. When your life is tallied, you will be asked for an explanation. If your life is close to achieving its major goals, but you did little for others, you will return. That is a fact. If you are unable to independently clear the final hurdle, helping others who are struggling to achieve their goals could help you achieve yours. It is not definite, but it helps.

When the work of God is done on Earth, and Earth is not needed, you will be told about it, but you will not be told why. It is not your business to know why. The world always asks, "Why?" We are not asking—and you will not ask. You will do what you must do. It is not a choice. It is a command to be heeded or you die and return for another round. Why? You ask. Why is not important, but the attitude with which you seek to know the meaning of God is.

You are often too brash and bold. You do not realize you are unworthy of an answer. You are egotistical and naïve after a lifetime on Earth, and not at all mature. We see it, but you do not. If you could, would you change?

If it would help even one of you to seek God, we would help you see what we see, but it is too laborious a proposition. You do not have enough time. When you come to understand the narrow parameters in which you operate, you will see how difficult it is to help a single person when so many are in dire need of direction and instruction.

The work of many is seen, but to merely watch is unworthy of you. You seek entertainment in order to avoid work you must do to provide a safe future for yourself. You seek out those who are unable to cope—in order to feel superior, but they are trying and you are not. You will not gain anything from sitting in a group and talking. You must move into the light of day or moon and talk to God. It is not difficult to do, but you cannot do it as a committee. *You* are alone!

When the work of a few is deemed superior, you can identify with them. If the work of the superior is not acclaimed—as is the case in your world today, you have no basis to confront your own work and compare your labor to the best. We suggest work of superiors be allowed to stand as is without judgment by you and other mortals.

If something deserving of credit is discredited, you are denied the ability to achieve your own worth. You are lost. Let no one condemn another for working on what is his or her way to worship God. It is not for you to judge!

God does not ignore the work of a single person, but man continually overlooks the best. You must not be discouraged or downhearted if the world does not recognize your work as good. It is enough that you know it is your best work. God will recognize that stirring in your breast as esteem rising from a job well done.

Whatever you do, do it as you would do the last work of your life. If you sincerely believe this is the last job you will ever have, you do it with sincerity and verve—and put your best effort into it. That is the way of the master.

You will be a master. You will not require the applause of minor actors in the play you directed. Your play is written, directed, and acted by only one—*you!* You are the star!

When you seek out the best in others, we seek out the best to help you. If you seek out only those who make you look good by comparison, we do not bother to send you help. It is not that we discriminate, but you do. If you know what you are doing and can do it, do not seek out help. To seek out help in order to demonstrate how you work is not the way to enlightenment. You will only slow your progress if you do.

The student presents herself or himself to the teacher, not the other way around. Your own ways of doing things are your ways, but if someone wishes to learn your ways, it is required that you show them. You must never deny anyone knowledge you worked to gain, but do not pursue the student and relinquish all right to your own life.

When people stand before you and tell how they overcame life problems, they are testifying to the fact that they are still working on them. You are not to interfere with that process, instead seek out those no longer preoccupied with such things.

In the world of your people today, many assign themselves the role of teacher and adopt a pedantic attitude, going publicly from place to place asserting themselves on all who will listen. We do not approve. We see the ego as still apparent and will not be stilled until that person learns to let students come forward and seek.

You are not teachers, but you do tutor others. We are not tutors, nor do we think you need to be tutored, but it is a role many are suited to now. A student may help another student. It is the only way some learn, but be sure you do not set yourself up as a teacher until you are called to be one. This is enough about the role you are to assume.

While we are here and able to help you, we will, but if you are unwilling to call upon our work and follow our teachings, we will not let that stop us from influencing those who work around you and through *you*. Many people learn from the bad example set by others, thus we will use bad lives of some as lessons. Be sure your life is not one of them!

While on Earth we want to freely look into things of great interest to you, but you are unable to reciprocate. The world of the *future* is closed to you—except on Earth planes. You have different parallel systems in operation. You live on one and dream on another, but you will never be fully aware of them all.

We see you do not believe you cannot know all there is, but that is true. While on Earth you are students. You will never be told everything, because you are not advanced enough.

When you move to the next highest plane and are there to stay, you will be able to manipulate how parallels intersect and combine. It is not the work of fools or idealists, but the work of your soul in harmony with other souls trying to redeem the work you did while on Earth. Your work on Earth is not complete until you leave this plane. Then you will know exactly why you were here and what you learned, as well as how you were instrumental in helping God develop souls.

Work is the only way for man. It is the way God prescribed for you to be *you*. If you laze about and seek idle people to associate with and never bother to improve your original lot in life, you will not be promoted. You will stay in this plane. Get busy! Do not let your work go.

We are here to help you get organized and get on with your work. We never discontinue the work of many in order for them to sit in idleness. You are the one who chooses to sit in idleness if an employer of many years disbands and does not provide you with work.

You are responsible for finding work. Work is not the wrath of God. It is God! You are known by your work. You are promoted on that basis. If you seek no one to help, and you do nothing, you will never know the feeling of being in charge. You will always fear. You will never be the one to create your life and what you want.

We see many fear you will end your lives in poverty, but that is nonsense. You are not to leave Earth and all you have worked for without a sense of accomplishment. If you do, indeed you are very poor; however, you cannot take material substance with you—only the spirit of your life, work, and friends.

While on Earth you also must get along with all you meet, regardless of where you meet, so be careful of where you go and whom you are likely to meet there. You will not run into drunkards at church or saints in bars. We exaggerate, but you get the picture!

What you do to others is also how you will be treated. Your life on Earth is a reversal of the negative at the end. Your picture is taken and the exposure either ends in a masterpiece or a failure. You can easily expose yourself. Only you will be able to erase a line or blemish—others cannot.

We will go into these last two areas once we are sure you totally understand you must work each and every day of your life if you are to advance spiritually. *Spiritually-oriented* people are often the first to refuse to work. We are not surprised, because we know they fear being harmed by exposure to the world—but that is why they are here. You will never know the world if you never work in it. The work of your hands is of Earth, and Earth is the workshop you chose.

If you do not succeed in the terms of your world, you are not a success. It is that simple! You have the ability to choose to be whomever you wish and do whatever you please, but you must work at it until you succeed. A person who works up to the last day on Earth is a success, regardless of how much they earn.

You know you will never be paid for all you do, but neither do you pay others for all they do, so it is a trade-off. We are not here to instigate a riot in the workplace, but many who work in the world do not labor. They supervise the work of others and defy the wrath of God by placing themselves over other people, but that is not your concern. You are to work.

We will return in due time for another lesson, but you need time to recapture the lost art of work. You need to believe the work you do is the most important thing you do. We leave you with that thought.

Chapter Seventeen

This is the time when the work of man ends and the beginning of the time when men will work. You are unable to work now, but soon you will all work. Your work is to be done, and if you have time, you will work for the good of all. This is the triumph. To be able to work for the good of all is the master's way of showering you with tribute from good times on Earth.

What you need now is the end of the old lifestyles and the advent of new, but it is so steeped in tradition that you cannot leave the past. You want to adapt and adopt various provisions from others; you do not want to invent anything. This is the reason your world is dying. You need to reinvent yourselves if you are to continue; and since so many of you are fully aware this is not the end of the line for your soul—and you wish to proceed, we cannot see the sense of your inventing a new world order now.

When your life is out of order, you call for a repairman. You do not look at it and try to dismantle your life. Instead, you sit and cry over having to pay money to someone to fix your possessions and your bodies. We want you to analyze what went wrong and why, and then try to fix it yourself. Only if and when you cannot fix it, call for help from your Spiritual

Guides. Your Spiritual Guides are not to be abused by hearing from you every day of your life. You need not call upon them to do what you can do yourself. You need to clear up details before seeking God's help.

As for personal Spirit Guides, we see you are not as familiar with them now as people in the past who called forth their Guides regularly. As times changed and evil invaded the world you created, Spiritual Guides took less and less from you, yet created no realm of their own.

Your body is the place in which your soul dwells. It is not just a body. It is a soul. Your body and soul are divided into two separate, distinct areas that control *you* and your physical needs as well as the spiritual advancement of your soul. This is a lesson you need to learn, but we have no time for it.

When you are together in a group, you often let one person dominate you all. This group activity is not good, because you need to gather and greet one another, but not as slaves who seek the good will of a master. You are all free. Not one of you has a master on Earth—you could, but you do not!

When the work of your hands is such that it does not please you, then you should change the work. Instead, you are too quick to change your minds. You often start several projects at one time, which is not the way to accomplish your life's goals.

Your life's goals are unknown to others. Your goals are yours alone and not to be trotted out for the general approval of others. We sense a delight on the part of some to show off to the world how advanced they are spiritually or psychically. We do not approve. You will know why later.

Without a lot of trouble, we will begin to seek out a lot of work for all reading this book. We will begin by searching your minds as you read. Is this too difficult for you to comprehend— that we can seek material and search your minds? We can, and it makes no difference when you tune into this material!

We will help all who ask for help. If it is your desire to pursue further education, let us know. We will honor all who make such a request from their heart; however, we will not bother with fools. God alone bothers with fools!

You are not to be one who calls people in order to bore them with commonplace details about your everyday life. So why call angels and Guides for trivial reasons? You never know if words you speak are heard? We hear all that is spoken aloud, but we do not impact upon your personal thoughts. You need not speak aloud if the intent is to reach only the ears of God, but for us to help *you*, we need to hear you speak aloud.

In the work of God there is a way that is not our way. It is the way of the patient plodder. We are quick and impatient. We strive to clear the air and water and educate the population now! We always try to correct your mistakes by pointing out how you can improve yourself, but God does not try to improve you. You will not be asked to correct mistakes. Your life will simply be judged as is.

When a teacher is good at his or her work, the world is

not aware of it. But if a teacher fails, the world can see it. You must do your work so well that no one knows you are good. We want you to manage to always be there for your students without intruding into their lives. We want you to help without imposing your methods. We want you to freely define and refine ideas, but not create. If this is contradictory, you are now aware of how difficult it is to teach.

A teacher who fails the student is cursed, but a teacher is blessed who promotes and advances a student who then succeeds. You must not let fear prevent you from projecting your beliefs. You must live your life, and if others ask for advice, you must give all you have. We are unable to drive numbers to the top of a chart to show how much a student advanced, but we know. Your help is calculated, and you will be advanced accordingly.

Never worry about the work of man being inferior to the work of God. It is never judged against such high standards. It is judged against the work of other men and never conveniently forgiven for being unable to take the time to do a good job. Excuses are not heard, only results are seen.

Your life is not made up of what you once said, but it does continue to reflect what you did. Records may be changed, but seldom are. You must take time to make sure your life is clear of any omissions. If you are unable to clarify work you have done, we suspect you did not do it, for only those who steal the work of others are unable to describe in detail its intricate inner workings.

If you do not believe in God, why bother to call your Guides to help you? We see some do that. We find it a curious and inexplicable exercise in contradiction. Why would you believe your Guides could help you to achieve a lifetime dream when you do not believe you have a life? We seek out such inconsistencies and draw your attention to them so you may examine yourselves.

In the world of your creation, we are not allowed to hold forth on religions of your invention, but we can explore them. You do not know of the ways of others, because you are sure your own way is the only way. As a result, you become intolerant and antisocial. This is a failing that can and will result in your expulsion from the next plane.

You must be able to get along with ALL people—not just your own kind. We are unaware of many on Earth truly caring about others. This begins in the home and is fostered by the religions of Earth. You will be called to task for this.

❧

If you say: "I do not believe."
You believe!

When you cannot explain something, your first reaction is to deny its existence. We see you are familiar with that concept and are prepared to argue, but do not deny it. We see you unable to recognize what you cannot believe, so you deny. It is the same idea.

We are not of flesh, but flesh is not as easy to use as the ethereal body you normally have. For this reason, we often grant you immunity. But you need to realize this does not excuse you from being true to *you*.

You do not have to live on Earth to be of Earth. We see you do not understand. Let us say this: You live on Earth, but there are those who also are of Earth and not seen by you. Those who dwell on Earth and are unseen by humans are not fairies, elves, gnomes, or whatever else. They are the only entities who can live in the same dimension as you and not be seen as intruding upon your lives, but they exist. You will not be bored now by our explanation of why you must not destroy the Earth, since it is home to other beings beside you. We will write of this another time.

What you need do is be true to the inner source of your life. If you are unhappy, it is because you lost your way. Once you are back on the path, you fear nothing. You are confident, happy, and able to help others find their way, too. That is our mission. We are here to help you get back on the right path.

Your life is unlike the life of anyone else. You are entirely different. You cannot liken yourself to anyone else. You cannot say you resemble anyone else, either. We see this disturbs you, but it is true.

Heredity is no excuse for abuse. You cannot say: "I abuse others because I was abused as a child." We will not tolerate such slander of the entities placed in charge of your upbringing. If indeed you were sorely abused, they will answer to God for that, but you have no right to say anything about them.

You are responsible for you and your offspring, but not responsible for the lives of your parents. If you do not treat properly with respect your parents or whoever raised you, you will be tortured by guilt. This guilt is often present in the minds of those who cannot free themselves of this world. They often linger at the end trying to recapture the war they imagined between themselves and their parents—in order to justify their behavior, but it is too late for that. No amount of dawdling at the end of life can change the ill-begotten behavior of a lifetime. It is best to end life quickly and prepare for the consequences.

Whether or not you can war is of no importance to us. We see only the ravages of your efforts to control others. We see no great accomplishments as the result of war. Your life may or may not be affected directly by a war, but it is of little consequence to us.

You are to be *you*. If you are in a war and act like a beggar and a thief, you are a beggar and a thief. If you act like a man or woman of integrity, you are such a person. The fact that you were caught up in a war is no excuse for your bad behavior or aggression toward another human being or beast. This is not good news for many of you, but it is important that you now take the necessary steps to improve your chances at the end of this life.

If you have done some great injustice and harmed another, you cannot freely flow into the next higher plane, but there are times when you may be allowed to advance. We now seek to advance souls who have harmed people. *This is indeed the main reason we are here now.*

If you hurt someone who trusted you, this is a far different crime than harming someone unintentionally. It can seldom be justified—even by the most adroit Spiritual Guides. You will be seen as you are. If this scares you, then begin at once to clear up the past and seek different work.

If you work hard every day to clear up a worthless past, you may be able to create a better life for someone else. This is always viewed as a beneficial way to work your way out of this life. Yes, you can work your way out of this life by doing good works for others, even if not valued by them. If you send a soul to grace and that soul is unable to see you helped, you still get credit. We see you. We are not imposing ourselves upon you, but we do report your actions. In the final decision, your life is held up to all the upper planes for review, and acceleration can happen if you are not of evil intent.

In the world you live in and created, there are some who have tried to imply God is second to another equally powerful being, but that is believed only on your plane. No one else in the universe is that dumb! We see you are shocked.

We are surprised that even a young person could dream up much evil, but it happens. You are who filled the child's mind, so you will be held responsible. Whether or not you care about a child is no excuse for not helping every child on Earth you come in contact with. As an adult you are always responsible for the well-being of children. You cannot say: "I was afraid of being coerced into raising the child; or I saw no reason to interfere." These are false and faint claims that result in another round in this earthly plane. So forget about abandoning a child, or pretending you do not see the war a child goes through, you are seen.

We are always of the same temperament whether or not you are happy or sad. Your earthly plane is not conducive to great happiness, but there are those who achieve it. It is a gift. You, too, may earn such a gift by being true to *you*, then it is yours.

We feel the presence of others around The Scribe as she is called to teach now, but we will regain our momentum and continue this lesson at another time. Be true to You!!

Chapter Eighteen

This is THE DAY—
WE ARE HERE!

THERE IS NO OTHER TIME BUT NOW. YOU ARE NOT OF THIS EARTH. YOU ARE SPIRITUAL BEINGS OF ANOTHER PLACE WHO HAVE BEEN ESCORTED TO EARTH TO FURTHER DEVELOP YOUR ABILITIES TO BE YOU AND TO BECOME THE BEST OF ALL.

IF YOU ARE UNABLE TO READ THIS BECAUSE OF THE UPPER CASE LETTERS, WE SUGGEST YOU SKIP TO THE NEXT SESSION. THIS SESSION IS FROM THE WORLD OF BUDDHA—AND BUDDHA ALWAYS SPEAKS IN A LARGE VOICE.

HOW DO YOU KNOW THE BUDDHA SPEAKS? YOU KNOW! YOU ARE THE ONLY ONE TO KNOW. WE DO NOT SPEAK OF YOU IN THE PLURAL, BUT YOU MUST SPEAK OF GOD IN THE PLURAL, SINCE GOD IS MANY IN ONE. YOUR LIFE IS NOT WORTH A LOT TO YOU, BUT IT IS WORTHY OF GOD. IT IS OF GOD. IT BELONGS TO GOD.

YOU ARE NEVER TO HURT YOURSELF OR CAUSE PAIN

TO ANY OTHER BEING, FOR YOU HURT THAT WHICH IS. WHEN YOU SEE THE WORK OF GOD, YOU SEE YOU. IF YOU CANNOT ACKNOWLEDGE GOD, YOU ARE NOT VALID EITHER. YOUR LIFE IS NOT OF WORTH TO YOU, BUT YOU ARE OF WORTH TO THE UNIVERSE.

FOR THIS REASON, WE SEEK YOU. IF YOU DOUBT IT, LET US SHARE WITH YOU THIS LITTLE STORY.

A MAN WENT INTO THE WORLD TO SEEK HIS SON AND FOUND ONLY A LITTLE BOY WHO KNEW HIM NOT. THIS LITTLE BOY WAS SO SORRY FOR ALL HE HAD DONE THAT HE LEFT THE MAN AND NEVER RETURNED. THE MAN LOOKED EVERYWHERE FOR THE BOY AND CRIED OUT HIS NAME, BUT HE NEVER HEARD HIM OR SAW HIM.

AFTER A FEW YEARS, THE MAN STOPPED LOOKING FOR THE BOY AND EVEN BECAME ACCUSTOMED TO BEING WITHOUT HIM—THEN THE BOY APPEARED. HE WAS AFRAID TO SHOW HIS FACE, BUT HE NEEDED THE MAN TO HELP HIM LIVE. HIS OWN LIFE WAS NOT AS HE HAD WISHED IT TO BE, AND HE BLAMED HIS FATHER FOR IT. THE MAN LET OUT A HOWL AND CHASED THE BOY FROM HIM. THE BOY RESPECTED THIS AND LEFT.

AFTER MANY YEARS THE BOY AGAIN APPROACHED THE MAN, ONLY THIS TIME HE DID NOT SAY ANYTHING. HE LET THE MAN ASK HIM QUESTIONS. THE MAN ASKED MANY QUESTIONS. HIS ANSWERS WERE NOT WANTING. HE WAS DEEMED AN HONORABLE MAN AND

WELCOMED BACK INTO THE ARMS OF HIS FATHER. THIS IS HOW LIFE IS.

WE ARE NOT AS YOU ARE. WE ARE NOT EVEN WITHIN YOUR IMAGINATION. YOU KNOW NOTHING! YOU ARE TOO INSIGNIFICANT TO BE ABLE TO IDENTIFY WITH US, BUT YOU DO. THIS IS A TERRIBLE WORLD YOU HAVE CREATED, AND NOW YOU BLAME US. YOU SAY IT IS THE WORK OF THE DEVIL. YOU SAY IT IS NOT YOUR FAULT. YOU SAY IT IS NOT THE WORLD THAT IS WRONG, BUT GOD. YOU SAY MANY STUPID AND VILE THINGS, BUT THE WORST THING IS TO BLAME GOD.

GOD ABOVE US IS IN COMPLETE POWER OVER ALL. YOU ARE NOT IN THIS WORLD TO BE A HUMAN BEING. YOU ARE HERE TO BE AN HONORABLE AND LOVING ENTITY THAT DEVELOPS INTO THE NEXT EVOLUTION AND FURTHERS THE WORK OF GOD.

IF THIS IS TOO DEEP, YOU NEED ONLY WADE INTO THE MIDDLE AND THEN LOOK TOWARD THE SHORE. YOU WILL SEE HOW DEEP IT IS THERE. WE WILL EXPLAIN EVERYTHING YOU NEED TO KNOW TO BE ABLE TO GROW AND DEVELOP INTO THE NEXT AREA OF WISDOM AND HONOR. YOU ARE NOW READY.

IN THIS WORLD ALL ARE NERVOUS NOW. EVERYONE IS CONCERNED OVER THE WAY CHILDREN REACT TO ADULTS AND THE ESTABLISHED ORDER. NO ONE IS ACTUALLY TAKING CARE OF THE CHILDREN, AND NO ONE CARES TO DO SO, BUT ALL SPEAK OF CHILDREN AS

BEING SMALL ADULTS WHO ARE CAPABLE OF MURDER, MAYHEM, AND ATTROCITIES.

YOU ARE NOT IN CHARGE OF JUDGMENT. YOU ARE NOT THE ONLY ENTITIES ON EARTH, AND YOU ARE NOT THE ONLY HUMAN BEING. YOU MUST LEARN TO LIVE AND BE KIND TO OTHERS. IF YOU DO NOT, YOU DIE.

THE WORK OF THIS WORLD IS NOT OVER, BUT THE WORLD IS UNABLE TO CONTINUE TO SUPPORT SO MANY PEOPLE. YOU MUST END THE TERRIBLE PERSECUTION OF MY PEOPLE. YOU MUST END THE POPULATION WHO ARE NOT WILLING TO GOVERN THEIR APPETITES, WHO FEAR NO ONE. THIS POPULATION IS NOT ABLE TO GOVERN EVER AND WILL NEVER FREQUENT THE HIGHER PLANES IF THEY ARE NOT DISCIPLINED NOW. THE ENERGY GIVEN OFF BY SUCH NEGATIVE ENTITIES IS HURTING THE WORK OF GOD.

YOU WILL SEE THAT GOD DOES NOT FREQUENTLY CALL OUT TO THE WORLD, BUT THIS IS SOON TO BE CHANGED. GOD IS READYING HIS ANGELS AND ARCHANGELS, AND THE SOULS OF THOSE DEPARTED ARE ANGRY. WHETHER OR NOT YOU BELIEVE, YOU WILL BE CONCERNED. YOU WILL HAVE TO PAY A PRICE AND THAT PRICE IS NOT EASY TO RAISE IF YOU ARE UNABLE TO PAY. THE PRICE OF FREEDOM IS NOT LIFE, BUT THE FREEDOM TO LIVE. YOU WILL KNOW THE DIFFERENCE.

IN THE WORLD OF ENERGY AND FREEDOM, YOU ARE AN ENTITY OF DELIGHT, BUT NOT IN HUMAN FORM. THE HUMAN FORM IS CONFINED TO EARTH. IT CANNOT GROW BEYOND THE ESTABLISHED BOUNDARIES. YOU ARE FORCED TO CONFORM TO THIS LIFE OR DIE. IF YOU DO NOT CONFINE YOUR PASSIONS, YOU DIE.

IF YOU EAT LESS OF THE GROUND AND MORE OF THE MEAT, YOU DIE TOO SOON. IF YOU EAT OF THE AIR AND NOT THE GROUND, YOU DIE. YOU WILL NEVER WORK ON THE EARTH IF YOU ARE NOT GROUNDED IN THE EARTH. WE SEE YOU ARE CONFUSED. YOU ARE UNABLE TO EAT AIR, YOU SAY. THAT IS NOT CORRECT. EVERYTHING YOU EAT IS MADE OF AIR. MUCH OF THE TIME YOU EAT ONLY AIR. THERE IS NOTHING OF NUTRITIOUS VALUE IN IT? OH, NOW YOU SEE.

WHEN EARTH IS ON ITS WAY TO EXTINCTION—AND IT IS NOW, YOU WILL SEEK SHELTER, BUT THERE IS NONE. YOU LIVE ONLY HERE. HOW CAN YOU LIVE ON ANOTHER PLANET? THIS IS THE ONLY PLACE WHERE OXYGEN AND HYDROGEN ARE PLENTIFUL ENOUGH TO SUSTAIN YOUR BODIES. YOU CANNOT ESCAPE. YOU MUST LIVE HERE. THIS IS THE LESSON.

NOW THAT YOU FULLY COMPREHEND THAT YOU CANNOT ESCAPE FROM EARTH, AND YOU CANNOT LIVE WITHOUT AIR AND WATER, WHAT ARE YOU GOING TO DO?

THE FIRST THING TO DO IS TO SEEK A WAY TO CLEAN THE AIR AND WATER. IT IS NOT IMPOSSIBLE, BUT IT REQUIRES COOPERATION. COOPERATION IS ALMOST TOTALLY GONE. THIS IS THE RESULT OF MISERLY WAYS AND OVER-COMPENSATING THE FEW AT THE EXPENSE OF THE MANY.

YOU WILL NEVER BE ABLE TO RELINQUISH THE FEAR. IT IS INHERENT IN ALL YOU DO. WHEN YOU FEAR, YOU CAUSE THE WORK OF GOD TO BE SHALLOW AND COARSENED. IF YOU DO NOT FEAR, YOUR EYES ARE OPENED TO ALL THAT GOD HAS PREPARED. IT IS THE REWARD OF THE WORLD. YOU MUST BEGIN TO OPEN YOUR EYES AND FEAR NO ONE. THIS IS THE ONLY WAY TO LIVE. TO DO OTHERWISE IS TO GIVE UP.

WE ARE REACTING TO YOU, AND WE SEE YOU SHIRK THE RESPONSIBILITY. YOU DO NOT WISH TO HELP. THAT IS THE WAY OF MEN. THAT IS THE WAY OF THE WORLD. THAT IS NOT THE WAY OF GOD. YOU MUST CHANGE!

WE ARE NOT HAPPY TO BE THE ONES TO CHALLENGE YOU. YOU ARE UNABLE TO UNDERSTAND THIS. YOU FEAR, AND THEN YOU SHRUG IT OFF. YOU ACCEPT, AND THEN YOU GO BACK TO THE OLD WAYS. YOU DO NOT THINK! IF YOU WOULD, YOU COULD SEE THAT THE TIME IS NOW RIPE FOR A PURGING—AND IT IS NOT GOD'S WORLD, IT IS YOUR WORK. YOU CREATED THE WORLD, AND GOD CREATED EARTH. KNOW THE DIFFERENCE AND MAKE YOUR PEACE.

IN THE DARK OF THE MOON YOU SEEK OUT THE EVIL OF PEOPLE, BUT YOU DO NOT SEEK IT OUT IN THE SUN. YOU WAIT UNTIL DARK. THAT IS THE HABIT OF THE PAST, BUT IN THE FUTURE ALL WILL SEEK OUT EVIL AT ANY TIME.

THE SUN IS UNABLE TO SHINE. THE MOON IS NOT SEEN. THE EARTH IS THICK WITH SMOKE, AND THE WORK OF MAN IS OVER. THIS IS THE TIME TO BEGIN. DO NOT WAIT UNTIL THE SUN IS NO LONGER WARM.

WE SEND YOU GREETINGS, BUT WE ALSO SEND YOU A WARNING. YOU MUST BE WISE ENOUGH TO UNDERSTAND THE DIFFERENCE. IF YOU SHARE YOUR WISDOM, MANY OTHERS WILL BE SPARED; BUT IF YOU KEEP IT TO YOURSELF, YOU WILL SUFFER THE CONSEQUENCES. LIFE IS NOT AN ISOLATED PROJECT WHERE YOU LIVE AS YOU WISH. IT IS A WORLD WHERE ALL MUST LIVE TOGETHER, AND IT IS NOT EASY TO LIVE IF THERE IS NO PEACE. YOU MUST RESTORE HARMONY.

THE EARTH IS FULL OF ITS WASTE. YOU HAVE SCRATCHED ITS SURFACE AND DEFILED ITS WATER, AND NOW YOU FILL UP THE INSIDE WITH WHAT GREW OUTSIDE AND EXPECT MIRACLES. YOU ARE BEING FOOLISH. KNOW IT AND ACT ACCORDINGLY.

WHEN THE WORLD IS DONE AND ALL ARE GONE, DO YOU SEE THAT THIS WAS A MISTAKE? DO YOU THINK GOD SHOULD HAVE PREPARED YOU BETTER? DO YOU

THINK YOU HAD TOO MUCH ATTENTION OR NOT ENOUGH? WE ARE SURE YOU THINK OTHERS HAD MORE ADVANTAGES THAN YOU DID, BUT YOU HAVE HAD ALL YOU NEEDED. IF YOU ARE NOT ENDOWED WITH BEAUTY, BE ASSURED YOU HAVE SOME OTHER VALUABLE RESOURCE TO DRAW UPON. IF YOU HAVE INHERITED NO MONEY, YOU CAN BE SURE YOU HAVE MANY WAYS TO EARN IT. THE WORLD IS NOT AT ALL STACKED AGAINST ANY ONE PERSON, BUT IT IS WASTED BY MOST. YOU WILL KNOW.

WE ARE TIRED OF THE WORK OF THE WORLD. WE CARRY OFF THE WORK OF MANY AND DISPLAY IT TO THE HIGHER PLANES, AND THEY SEE YOU ARE FOOLS. THIS IS NOT WHY YOU ARE HERE! YOU ARE HERE TO ENJOY LIFE AND BUILD A BETTER LIFE FOR FUTURE GENERATIONS. IF YOU LOSE THIS SENSE OF IDENTITY AND CARING, YOU LOSE. THE WORK OF THE PREVIOUS GENERATION WAS EXCELLENT. THEY BROUGHT FORTH MANY GREAT INVENTIONS THAT EASED THE SUFFERING AND WORK OF OTHERS. BUT THE CURRENT GENERATIONS ARE USING UP THOSE SAVINGS AND DELIVERING THEMSELVES INTO THE HANDS OF THE WICKED.

THIS IS THE ONLY TIME WE INTEND TO PREACH. YOU WILL HEAR US OUT! THIS IS NOT EARTH, BUT YOUR WORK. YOU ARE NOT ON EARTH TO BE A HERO OR HEROINE, BUT YOU ARE HERE TO HELP AND PROVIDE FOR ALL WHO ARE IN NEED. IF YOU ARE SELFISH AND

INDIFFERENT, YOU RUN THE REAL RISK OF BEING IN NEED YOURSELF. IF YOU DO NOT CARE FOR THE WORLD, YOU STILL HAVE TO LIVE HERE. IT IS STILL YOUR JOB TO PROTECT THE POOR AND DOWNWARD BENT.

YOU ARE NOT FREE TO LEAVE AND ENTER THE NEXT PLANE. YOU HAVE TO TAKE CARE OF THE DETAILS. YOU HAVE TO CLEAR THE AIR AND WATER. YOU HAVE TO HELP THE WORK OF GOD BECOME ESTABLISHED AND REESTABLISHED. IF YOU DO NOT, YOU WILL REGAIN ALL OF THE NEGATIVE ASPECTS YOU HAD PRIOR TO THIS INCARNATION. YOU WILL HAVE GAINED NOTHING FROM THIS LIFE. YOU WILL HAVE TO REINCARNATE. YOU WILL HAVE TO SUFFER THE SINS OF YOUR OWN LIFE NOW, AND THIS IS HELL!!

IN THE HELL OF YOUR IMAGINATION YOU SEE THE WORLD AS BEING THE END OF THE LINE, BUT IN REALITY HELL IS YOUR MIND AND YOUR BODY HAVING TO REPEAT AND REPEAT AND REPEAT UNTIL IT CAN MUSTER THE ENERGY TO GO FORWARD. MANY ON EARTH ARE HERE TODAY TO RELIVE THE PAST, BUT NOT ALWAYS TO RELIVE AN EVIL OR NEGATIVE EXPERIENCE—EVEN THOUGH EARTH IS NOT THE FAVORITE RESIDENCE OF ANY ENTITIES OTHER THAN HUMANS. SOME ARE HERE TO HELP. SOME ARE HERE TO TEACH. SOME ARE HERE TO OBSERVE.

IN THE END OF YOUR TIME, YOU WILL LEARN WHO WAS HERE TO HELP, WHO WAS HERE TO TEACH, AND WHO WAS HERE TO OBSERVE. YOU WILL NOT KNOW

UNTIL THEN, AND THEN IT WILL BE TOO LATE. FULLY UNDERSTAND THAT ANYONE WHO INTERFERES WITH ANYONE SENT HERE TO COMPLETE A MISSION IS IN GRAVE DANGER. YOU MUST NEVER FIGHT WITH ANGELS! YOU MUST NEVER GIVE CONFLICTING STORIES TO OBSERVERS. YOU MUST HELP. THESE ARE THE ONLY RULES.

EVERYONE CALLS UP TO SEE IF THEY ARE DOING WELL, BUT NO ONE IS. YOU ARE ALL AFRAID OF THE DAY WHEN YOU WILL DIE BECAUSE YOU ARE UNABLE TO FREE YOURSELF OF FEAR. THE FEAR OF DEATH IS WHAT BINDS ALL OF YOU TOGETHER ON EARTH. IT IS NOT KNOWN ANYWHERE ELSE. YOUR DEATH IS NOT A TERRIBLE EXPERIENCE. YOUR BIRTH WAS VERY DIFFICULT, BUT DEATH IS NOT.

IF YOU SEEK TO KNOW MORE ABOUT DEATH, DO NOT ATTEMPT TO EXPERIMENT AND SEE IF YOU CAN DIE AND RETURN. THIS IS SUICIDE AND SUICIDE IS NOT A WAY TO SEE GOD. YOU WILL NOT SURVIVE IF YOU DO NOT LET UP ON THE EXPECTATION THAT YOUR LIFE IS THE ONLY ONE THERE IS. YOU MUST RECOGNIZE THIS FACT AND GET ON WITH YOUR LIFE. IF YOU ARE STILL UNABLE TO GRASP THIS VERY SIMPLE CONCEPT, YOU CANNOT CREATE A NEW LIFE ON A HIGHER PLANE.

IN THE WORK OF GOD IS THE WORLD OF MAN, BUT THE WORLD OF MAN CANNOT CREATE GOD GOD IS!

WITHIN THE NEXT FEW MONTHS OF YOUR LIFE YOU WILL SEEK TO BE BETTER, BUT HOW LONG WILL IT BE BEFORE YOU ARE? YOU ALONE CAN CUT THE DISTANCE TO ENLIGHTENMENT. WE ARE NOT HERE TO HELP YOU. WE ARE HERE TO TEACH YOU. THERE IS A BIG DIFFERENCE. YOU SHOULD KNOW THAT ALREADY, BUT IF YOU DO NOT, YOU WILL SEE IT NOW.

HELPERS ARE UNAWARE THEY ARE HERE TO HELP, BUT IF THEY ARE AWARE, THEY CAN WORK FASTER. LOCATE YOUR SPIRITUAL GUIDES AND SEE IF YOUR PURPOSE ON EARTH IS TO HELP. IF IT IS, THEN BEGIN IMMEDIATELY. YOU WILL BE HELD RESPONSIBLE FOR NOT DOING ENOUGH IF YOU DELAY. THE WORLD NEEDS HELP!

WHATEVER YOU DO, DO IT WELL. DO NOT ACT LIKE YOU ARE BORED AND TIRED OF WORK, THAT IS NOT THE WAY TO REACH SECURITY OR ENLIGHTENMENT. YOU WILL BE PUNISHED IF YOU DO NOT WORK. IT IS THE LAW. YOU ARE HERE TO WORK HARD EVERY DAY. YOU HAVE BEEN TOLD.

AS FOR GETTING ALONG WITH OTHERS, MANY ARE NOW FAR AHEAD OF US. WE SEE YOU WORK IN GROUPS TO GENERATE ENERGY IN ORDER TO PERSUADE OTHERS AND HELP THE WORLD HEAL ITSELF, BUT TOO MANY MORE ARE NOT. YOUR WORK IS ONLY BEGINNING. YOU MUST HEAL THE EARTH AND CONTINUE TO HELP, BUT WE SEE IT AS NOT LASTING. IF YOU DO YOUR PART, REGARDLESS OF THE FINAL

OUTCOME, YOU ARE REWARDED.

THIS IS THE END OF THE SERMON. WE WILL RETURN.

Chapter Nineteen

There are no days off!

〰

You work every day of your life. This is a law. You do get holidays or days of rest. On days when you do not work physically, you work spiritually, at about a proportion of one to three. If your days are long, then you must work less and meditate longer. If your days are short, you must work long and hard and meditate less. We are speaking of your life.

If you are young, you must meditate more than when you are old. It is the balance of youth and wisdom. Youth is developing wisdom, and age has it.

If you do little all day long, you sleep less. If you work hard and do all the chores and details assigned to do that day on that day, you sleep free of concern. We see many DO NOT work hard now, and you do not continue your work of the previous day. This is very wasteful. You need to continuously apply pressure to a spot if it is to stop bleeding. If you let up, it flows freely. This is the same as the energy of your body. If you let up applying pressure, you will be sapped of all your strength and have accomplished nothing.

Wherever several people of like mind gather, we are. We seek out the two or three women—even men at times—who discuss spiritual work. If they are on the right track, we give them energy to pursue it. We inspire so they can perspire! This is the feeling you get after a long, hot day when the work is done and you know you did it all well.

If your work is not going well, change it. You are in total control of your life. It does influence others, but basically it is not important to anyone else. You must forget the notion that you are an integral part of a greater being. You are a part of that being, but not the center. You will not be missed. If this is harsh, you must know it in order to move ahead.

You are not to be remembered for anything you said or did if it was not of great spiritual worth to others. No one remembers hard work on the physical plane. It must reach up and into the spiritual realms to make an impression.

In the days ahead of *you*, we are able to help, but it is your call. You never call? You will never hear a response. That is how it works. You have to be ready for *a call*. If you have never received *a call* from God, you are not ready. It comes only after a long search and seeking within You.

What you seek is not of this world, but you must seek it in this world. We are unaware of the need for anyone in the end to be a big star, but all of you must seek success. You need to be assured that what is coming is not the end. It is the beginning of another aspect of your soul's development. It will be a great day!

Now all of you wonder why the last session was written in all capital letters. We are not alone. We are now joined by The Buddha. You see, The Buddha is ever-increasing in presence in your cultures, because *the way* is now open. If it had continued to be male dominated, The Buddha would be unable to appear. Many women in America see The Buddha now, but few men do. It is somewhat paradoxical, because the last years of The Buddha were not spent in this world but on the next plane. The Buddha is not as is depicted, but rather a great and glorious being.

If you seek The Buddha, you may not find a man. You seek no one and often find The Buddha. This is being done. If the work of your hands is big, you have much energy. This energy attracts The Buddha and followers of Buddha. You will know.

The Scribe has had several instances wherein The Buddha's presence was made known, and it was of great interest to her and those around her. In most cases, those with her were women. This is to teach the egos of today's Buddhists that they overlook the inner life of women and seek to return as men—which is not the highest level of development on the Earth plane. If you are to reach the highest level of enlightenment, you must experience your last life as women do. This does not exclude men—it merely readjusts them.

In ages past, all was physical, and men excel in the physical realm. In the future, all the work is spiritually-oriented, and women excel in this realm. Most women, but not all, have had experience being men. Some are here on Earth for a very short time, or it may be their first time, so they are not that far along;

but if a woman has reincarnated many times as a man and can integrate those fears into the being of a woman, wisdom is great. This is the reason oracles are women of older years. We seek such women.

In your culture it is unwise to praise women. You hate to be called sexist, but your culture is matricidal. You do not honor the women whom you were once a part. You do not honor the father or mother of your youth. These are failures that will result in a less than honorable work for your next incarnation. You must not let another day pass without honoring the life of your parents—even if they failed by your standards. You are judged by the harshness with which you judge others.

Whatever you do or where you go, seek great depth. Do not simply look, but study. Read, listen, watch, and acknowledge those who help you. This is the path to enlightenment.

We cannot manage much of the work you do, because we are not in flesh, but we can do it. However, you cannot manage our work. In the work of man is a great deal of war and conflict. We see you are not as you think you may be. You are sure you are peaceful and others are in conflict with you, but it is you who wars—not everyone else. If you do not war and cause conflict, there is none within you.

It is you who deal your cards—not the dealer. You are who have a lot of enemies—not your enemies. If you are unhappy, you alone are not happy. It is not because of the life you have, it is because you choose to be unhappy.

When you gamble, and many of you are now into it, we see you flex your intuitive muscle and try to guess the throw of dice or the deal of a card. It is an exercise that produces fools. It is not the work of a spiritual being. Your life is spent idling with fools, and you become whomever you associate with. It is the same with anything. Be careful of your companions, because they are you!

If this world is not to your liking (and it is not), then why do you continue as before? Why do you work at the same old work and play the same old games? Why are you so sure you know when the work you do is not *your* work? If you do not work on you, who is going to do it? It cannot be done by anyone else. You are going to be called to task at the end of this life episode; so if you care about incarnating and being relieved of this burden of flesh, you must do your work and do it now.

In the work of your mind you are free to be whomever you choose to be—and you are aware of that. You daydream and dream and ask for relief from pressure, but you are who applies pressure to *you*. No one else can. You are the real *you*, and no one else can move in and take over or adopt your soul. You are incapable of giving up your soul to another. That is idle superstition that prevented many from meditating, and will cause some people much trouble for having promoted such blasphemy.

Meditation is the source of divine wisdom. If you never pray or meditate, you are not wise. Thus you will never be able to reach the highest level of being on this plane, and you will be unable to react to the new world to come.

You must prepare for the new day. It is the time when human life will evolve into its next phase—and is preparing to do so within the next few months of time. We see you are unaware that time does not exist anywhere but on Earth. Time, as you mark it off, does not make sense to us, but we will use your concept. A month is long--but short. A year is a long time and seldom ends as it begins, but a month is over before anything begun at the beginning is done by the end, so we use a month to describe many things.

Whatever you want, you have. Whatever you do not want is over the next hill. You keep yourself in the area you wish to live. You may live anywhere in the world, but you choose to live where you are. If the time comes to move, move. No one else cares if you move.

Whatever is on the day's agenda, you are not the only one doing it. You reside with others and are responsible for your children, so be careful of any change that might upset them; otherwise, be gone and do what you love.

We are not concerned that your life will be shortened. You are. You think you will die before you get everything done, but you usually end your days in idleness. Why do you sit at the end of life? Why do you let others govern you then? We see many have reached a state of vegetation long before their bodies, and we see you may also fit into that mold.

Begin now to adopt the policy that you will be busy. You will work all the time on you. You will increase your knowledge, skills, income, lifestyle, and you will help all who need help and ask for it. This will fill all the days of your life, and your life will end in joy.

When the work of the day is over, and you are calm and relaxed, begin to seek the Lord of Night and Day and let the work fall from you. If you are still working when the day is over, proceed to the next level of activity before reviewing that day's work. You need a buffer zone to keep the energy in its proper place.

If your energy is low, keep it close to you
If your energy is high, give it out
~ This is the law ~

It will not harm you to give up energy, but it can harm you to keep it. We are aware you never feel such energy as energy. You feel it as enthusiasm, wealth, or power. We suggest you reveal the source of your energy to no one. Let others travel the road to self-discovery. Do not attempt to tell them how to live their lives.

We are drained. We have given a lot today. We are tired. We will not be as interesting because of this fatigue, so we go.

Chapter Twenty

This is not the end of the world!
You are not the end of the line!

We may have given you that impression, but this is not the end. You are to be on Earth—millions are here and must be able to continue to develop. What is in jeopardy is Earth! The beautiful planet you use is in danger. You must be responsible for it. You were not given this planet to use for selfish purposes. You were told to go, multiply, and use all that the Earth contained, but you were never told to waste and use what belonged to others.

In the world in which you dwell, you are spiritual beings trapped within cumbersome clothing and flesh in order to teach you how to use your abilities to think and act. If you could manifest as easily as we do, you would have to be considerably less encumbered. For instance, if we think of something we would like to manifest and make happen, it is! If you visualize and put all your energy into manifesting it, it can take as long as two years to arrive! That is not long on Earth, but very long to us.

In the next few years the path will be broadened and the way made clear for those who have great difficulty remembering why they are here. We are *The Teachers* and we see even now how many express a desire to know why they are here. You are suddenly aware this is a classroom—not the ultimate achievement of a lifetime. You are also aware you do not know much. This is the biggest step toward gaining wisdom.

You must lose the ego. The ego, as we see it, is nothing. It is the Earth work you are here to complete—and not much else. Once you leave Earth it is of no further use to you, so we suggest you learn to curb it now.

Within the world you live are many beings. You are only one of many humans, but there are many others who thrive and flourish in the same space. We talk to them and achieve a consensus. We hear their complaints and try to arbitrate, but it is growing difficult.

You are not the humans who were once sent here. You have developed into a race unto yourselves. This is the real difficulty in leaving this plane. You are so sure you exist and God is of no great importance that you are now unable to release your soul. You cling and cry out to be spared. You snivel and creep into the dark. You wish to be no part of the light of God.

When the world is gone and no one else is to be developed, God will be there to say why it is over. It is not up to us. We have no need to know and have no right, but humans demand, demand, demand to know everything. You are egoists! You think only of yourselves. You care not for birds, animals, and fields of flowers. You take and destroy. This is not the way of God!

To eat meat is no sin. It is the best way to build blood. You need it for blood, because blood is what makes you human. If you abstain from meat, you must be very careful to eat things that constitute blood. We see a radical difference in the substance of many of you. You are not eating properly. You are purposely eating little meat, but eating no meat does not make you healthy.

Meat is not evil, and the killing of animals for food is not evil. It is the killing of animals and not eating the meat that is evil. To kill a wolf is evil, because humans do not eat wolves and wolves do not eat humans. Wolves keep the animal population under control.

Humans are not to keep the animal population under control. Humans cannot keep their own kind under control, so why would God grant them the right to kill animals, birds, and fish to control them? If the animal is killed for food, you may wear the skins of that animal. If the animal is raised for no other purpose but to line the pockets of traders, it is evil. We are aware this evil is being corrected.

Since you are not the only being on Earth, we understand you are interested in knowing who else is here. We will underline this: <u>We are here to live and let live, but you are here to learn. You are **not** here to question and devise ways of avoiding work.</u>

If you are interested in why others are using your space, it is not your place to demand to know. If we are here to show you how to get on with your soul's journey, we can and will show and share much that we know, but you may not question our source or our intent. It is not of the world—that is all you need to know. The rest is ours to know.

When you start to learn, you often ask: "Why? How is this so?" But as you learn, you respect the fact that you know nothing. So how can you ask intelligent questions? Many of you are intelligent enough to ask questions now, but do not. However, many are unaware you have a spiritual life, yet ask stupid questions constantly. Which category do you fall into now?

In the world all is peace and quiet once the light appears, but after dark all is uprooted and evil takes the force of good and uses it to its own advantage. Evil does not thrive in the light—nor does it thrive otherwise. You fear *evil*. Evil has no power. You have power! If you choose to use it against another human, you are evil, but the act itself is not evil. There is no such thing as *evil forces*.

God alone reigns, and there is no time when God fought for good and lost. This is fiction devised by man to insure his ways would be heeded. It is a false doctrine that is not to be continued. You must stamp it out wherever you find it. In the works of the world, you are not the best and most cherished of all. You are one of many works of God—and God cherishes all.

We are here to dictate a new way of working. You are to try once again to regain what you have lost. You are to do your own work. You are to reign over the Earth, but not despoil it. You are to act like a lord, but not *THE LORD*.

If you require help, ask aloud and your Spiritual Guides will accept the challenge and seek all you need. Do not call upon God's angels to help you. If you need them, your Guides will call them. To call angels, who are above you, is blasphemy. You are not above anyone. You are students. You may not question the authority of those who are placed above you. On Earth you have lost your way and authority is questioned, but not in the upper planes. You will have to unlearn this bad behavior.

In the times to come all is well above and below. We will never again enter this realm once we leave. The work we do is not a long-term assignment. We are here to move you to the next plane and be gone. If you wish to know more about us, we can say this: We are here to teach. We love and admire you, but we are here now to help and teach you how to gather your forces and act in a responsible way in order to leave Earth.

We have no identity you could recognize, and we are not here to direct you to the final destination. We recognize your soul, but you cannot see us. We are not in flesh at any time, and we do not assume your roles. If you try to see us, you waste time.

It is not necessary to see. The sightless are gifted beyond anyone who has sight. So why do you suffer and worry about the loss of sight? Being blind does not refer to being sightless. You are all blind now—not just the sightless!

If you cannot stand the work you do, it is because you are unsuited to it. You must change it. If you are not married and desire to be married, you must marry. If you are married and unable to be *you*, then you must not remain married. It is so simple to us, but you all act like these are major problems. Why?

The work of your world is unlike that of any other. You are not the only ones who care about the development of your souls, but you are the only one unable to see how much there is. This is the source of much of your trouble in seeking enlightenment: You think this is it! This little planet and its inhabitants are far from being the only place in the universe where humans dwell—and little is known about them by you, but we know. This is the only planet, however, being destroyed.

When you destroy a planet, and it has been done before, you lose. You are not promoted. You are cast into the next world, which is not the best way to advance. You are unsuited for much once you leave Earth. You have much study to do before you can advance to the higher planes. If while on Earth you studied and prepared for the next life, you are ahead of the crowd, but you are not going to jump over them.

Many are not ready
But think they are
You are not!

❧

We are here to help you think everything you do not know, rather than require you to recite all you know. The Earth is not a classroom for fools. You have advanced to this level. You are not here to learn the basics. You have already mastered them, but are not advanced enough to be in charge of anything. You are like teenagers. You are not adults. You do not know enough to supervise and determine the destinies of others, but there are those who believe they are entitled to much. We seek them out and correct them most.

In the work of God are many things to do. You must be prepared to handle and do at least one thing well. If you do not, you cannot run up the ladder to the next level and have to stay and work on it again and again, if necessary—but now there is no time left. You must move on!

Wherever you go, you are wanted. If you go into the dark and are shot at by a fiendish person, you are not killed. You are merely slain. If the slayer is not caught and is permitted to live, the life of the slayer is stopped from progressing any further. This results in that person reincarnating. We must prevent such slayings from going unpunished if we are to slow the rate of reincarnation. This is something that can be done by humans. Do it!

If your life is not fully developed and you are unhappy, we can see that; but if you are happy and complain about it, we cannot see why you are upset. This results in a mixed message. If you complain, do you get more attention? We do not give you more attention as a result of complaining. Your legitimate complaints may also be ignored if you constantly talk about imagined woes. Some of you were told to never talk about the good you have accrued—this is wrong, but you must not complain.

When you can understand the work of God, you understand man. If you never grow, you will never know. The words of God are not written down, but the words are here. You can read them everywhere. We see you work and strive to correct old manuscripts, but why? The old work was for that age and you do not live in the past, you live NOW. If you want to seek the hand of God, read the papers you already have.

We see lives spent pursuing the past, but why do it? Why are you so interested in *past lives?* You cannot change them, or even live in them for a short time, so why do you ask about them? We do not care to discuss the reasons you came back to Earth. It is not why we are here. You came back to be here for some special reason and that reason is not buried in some past life episode. It is within you now.

If your life is not as you like, we will help you change it. But if you like your life, change happens anyway. Change is the only way to grow. You will not grow as long as you are stagnant, so welcome change and let it go. Do not try to hold onto the past.

Whatever the day, whatever the hour, you are the only one here who cares about *you.* That is the nature of man. You are not here to care for anyone else except you and any children you may bring into the world. The child is not responsible for you, but the child will take responsibility if you taught that to the child. You will reap exactly what you have sown!

Many of you complain that your children turn on you and act like animals and are disrespectful, but that is how *you* raised them. They are not you, but they reflect your teachings. We are being held responsible for *you,* because you are our student. All teachers are held responsible for the advancement or lack thereof of their students.

Many today are trying to avoid the final tally, but it is too late to worry about the past. If you failed your mission, you will be given another one. Do not fail the next one, because there is little time left on Earth. Whatever you do and wherever you go, it matters not; but if you do not work, you will be chastised severely.

Whatever you say and whenever you say it, we hear you. We do not bother with thoughts and ideas coursing through your brain. They are of no interest to us, but your voice raises vibrations that attract our attention, and we listen. Be sure your voice is not raised in anger. We may be able to seek out the anger, but you would not like that. All you say is not heard, but much of it is. We will never be concerned with idle gossip, but are concerned if it hurts another person. Your scorecard will reflect this, and you will be held accountable for it. You are not idly gossiping if the news is such that it would prevent another from falling victim to a fool, but it is idle gossip if it is motivated by jealousy or greed.

Now that we have finished our lecture, we see you are unable to clear your throat. Please do that and remember: We hear you!

Chapter Twenty-One

If the work of this world is not done, you must return. We are here to see that you understand this and work to stop your soul returning to Earth. Whatever you do and whoever you are, you are of God. This is a fact.

No one is ever forgotten or overlooked. No one is seen as less or greater than another. All have had their day in their universe. No one is going to be less for staying here, but you may not measure the effect of this time on Earth until you are off of it.

In the beginning, the work of this world was one of measuring, molding, and cutting the earth. Earth cannot be divided now. It is one world. It is not separate. It is the work of many, many generations of warriors and shamans. It is not the work of idiots, but the work is not progressive. It must be done over and over again. It is, after all, a classroom.

If the world is too new to you, you cannot see the flaws; and if the world is too old and tired for you, you are not gaining much. It is time to begin to move forward. The work of this world needs to be challenging and fulfilling. If the work of your hands is not growing and providing nourishment, then it is doing the opposite and must end.

We are not here to tell you how to live or what to do. We are here to develop a strategy that will enable you to leave Earth and move to the next plane. You have developed to this point, and to avoid growing is not to be condoned.

The Earth is not here for much longer. It has been destructively managed and abused by thousands of people who are no longer able to deliver themselves to the next plane. They are to be here until the end, in order to experience the results of their reckless behavior and inappropriate work against society for selfish ends. You may be one of them, but you will still be given a chance to leave.

If the world you know is not here, what will you do? We are aware of this materialistic world coming to the end. You are all calling for it to end now. It will be a matter of time, but it will end, and not as pleasantly as it began. The work of angels is to end one world and herald the beginning of another. We are not angels, and we are not here to herald the beginning of another world.

In the work of your hands is the work of God. If you wish to be a part of the world to come, you will be asked to help in the transition. This is beginning to happen now. Many are being called to do God's work, and many are answering that call. The Scribe who writes for us is only one of many.

If you are to do God's work, you must first want to do it. You must demonstrate the ability to work and develop yourself. If you remain interested in the world, you will be given a job that transcends and weaves its way between the two. If you wish to evolve and develop into a more spiritual work, you are welcomed, but this is not as likely to happen.

In the work of the world you are not *a* work. You create the work of the world. You create the world. You are the world! In the work of spiritual planes, you are not the work. You do not end the work. You do not begin the work. The work is God!

Whatever you do on Earth is your business, but the business of Earth is God's. You are not to be selfish and ignore the needs of one another, or you will be held back. This is like failure, but different. It is to teach you how to socialize and live with one another—and work together as one. If you cannot work as a whole, you will be unable to succeed.

This is the **Third Law of God**: *You must be able to get along with one another, and you must tolerate all others.* It is not necessary to love, but it helps. If you do not love, you are to at least help others. This is not a requirement of the world—but God.

When your life on Earth is over, we are not there to greet you. You are welcomed to the next plane after a time of examination and review by the inhabitants of that plane. This goes on over a long period until you reach the highest level of that plane and are ready to progress to the next plane.

Life on Earth is not a plane—it is a level. You are now at an advanced level and ready to make the transition to the next plane and are afraid. It is that simple. Change is frightening to humans. That is why you are here—to learn to trust.

When you fear, you set off an alarm heard on all planes, but only one responds—the next plane. We do not respond, because we are teachers. We are here to help your Guides accelerate your progress.

The task of Spiritual Guides is not going as well as in the past, because so many here are totally unaware of them. We are here to accelerate knowledge and gather up all the material you need to know in order to contact your Spiritual Guides. If you follow this material, you will be able to contact and maintain a daily conversation. This is to be given now:

1. In the initial stages of your life on Earth, you had daily contact with your Guides. You lived in the work of their work. That is to say, you were not fully developed, so you worked in their shadow.

    Then you grew into your world's teen years and became autonomous beings, you were to be given instruction in the ways of God at that time. However, the ways of God are not kept on Earth now—except by several small religious sects who believe they are the sole beneficiaries of God's work—and they are not.

    Once the work of the parent cannot be developed further, the child is then maturing and to be totally responsible for self; however, your societies now condone the passage of great time before an individual is required to be responsible for self. Lack of instruction and proper development of the young is now reaping negative input and resulting in wanton destruction. We will not let this go on any longer.

There is no work less important within the work of God, but to waste time and effort on foolish earthly pursuits is not the way to earn awards or *gifts*. We will talk of this later.

2. Once the entity is mature, the process of developing spiritually is not as difficult as before, but not that easy either. If you need help developing, you are not ready. You should be able to do the work and pursue the teacher, not the other way around. Once the student is aware of all that is unknown, the teacher is merely an instrument of God. All is known to God. All is God.

    You are now ready. You have pursued this work and done much work to reach this point. You are not alone. Your Guides are here as you read. We will help you call and ask for help and guidance. If you do not need help, you will obviously not need them; but if you get entangled or confused about a particular fact, call your Guides.

3. To call your Guides, you need only speak *aloud*. This is because your mind cannot cope with all the worldly activities you are mired in now. It causes a confusion of messages to be promoted and transmitted to us. We of the higher realms are unable to listen to such noise. It deafens and defeats us. We then tune it out and wait for conversation. If your conversations are inane, we tune them out, too; but if they are worthwhile, we often speak through you. This is what we call *'channeling'*.

    To channel is to speak in the words of the deity, but not the words of God. Only God speaks for God. No one can say he or she is a channel of God. Humans are unable to handle such tremendous power. We also are unable to do it. Only angels are permitted to announce and transform.

You are not to be confused now. We are *The Teachers*. You have your own Spiritual Guides. They are within You. You do not call upon angels. You call upon your Guides if you need help. This is the easiest way to get work done, but not the best.

Seek out your Guides only after you give a problem your intense scrutiny and have thought of all the ways it could be solved, only then call upon your Guides and ask for their help in deciding upon the best direction to take. If you hear nothing, wait. The work of your Guides is rapid, but often you ask for help with work that involves many others—which takes time, because your Guides cannot do it without seeking help and cooperation of others through *their* Guides.

Once your Guides reach agreement (there is usually more than one abiding with You), they will call *you*. If the answer is to be positive and helpful, *you* must be in a receptive mood; thus we ask you to meditate. If you are not quiet, you cannot hear your Guides. They will not intrude into your conscious mind. You must relax and clear your mind of all conscious matters. If possible, sit still and work on another problem. This preoccupation of the conscious mind frees you to accept inspiration channeled by your Spiritual Guides.

If Guides are unable to listen to you due to confusion in your mind, why do you think you can hear them? We are not here to go much deeper into this, but we will make one last point. You must learn to conquer worry. It is a negative thought pattern that prevents you from solving problems.

The work of your Spiritual Guides is never done. You came into the world with them and will leave the world with them. Your own work is always of interest to them, but not necessarily affected by them. They will not intrude as long as you are on the *right path*, but can be affected if you are not. If your path is not right for you, you will experience fatigue and irritation constantly. You will not like to be told of your shortcomings or need to be further educated. If you are on the right path, all is clear and you seek out those who would help you.

You never tire of doing your work, you are sure everyone is happy, too. If you are sure the entire world is unhappy—you are unhappy! You must begin to seek. You must change. In the end, the only way to be is to be *you*!

You came to Earth for a particular reason, and that reason is unknown to you until you are ready to pursue it. If you never pursue it, you will have to return to Earth. We want you to contact your Spiritual Guides now and ask for help in discovering why you are here and how you can make work such that you will not have to return again to complete it. With this information, you will have the best chance to complete your task.

In the end, the only work not to be considered is work of the world that was not required. You will not be judged on it. You are only judged on work you were sent here to do. So if you work only on the material aspects of life, you will be unable to pass on to the next plane. You will be expected to repeat and repeat this experience until you fully understand that life is life—*and no one on Earth is above God.*

In the work of this Earth, you are not the best nor the worst. You will not be judged on the degree of difficulty or the amount of time you spent on it. You will be judged by how much you accomplished. If it is done quickly, fine. If it takes all your life, fine. It is not the amount of time that counts; it is how much is done.

For anyone who has spent an entire life in the work of God, you are not to worry that your part is unappreciated. It is! You receive many blessings for being steadfast, and the greatest is that you will be honored among those who guided and helped you from above. The work of this world does not interest any above you, but your spiritual work does. We will not belabor this point, but since it is of great concern to some, we touched upon it.

In this session we had several interruptions. Our Scribe has been called away to attend to our people, but now is calm and able to channel for a longer period than usual. This is how you are, too. If you have to attend to the matters of the world, do so. You will lose no time, nor work harder when you return to your spiritual work, but your thoughts will be clearer.

The grounding that takes place while doing your daily work is most important. It causes a balance to occur between the air of your thoughts—which causes you to feel certain of yourself. If you cannot work, you feel dissatisfied. It is the fear of not being needed. You will experience that as long as you work for others.

In the end, you will work for *you*. This is the law of the land.

When you can assume full responsibility, you will end your indentured servitude and assume the role of employer. No longer are you beholden to the moods and whims of the employer, because you are now in charge. If you are an employee, you do not assume full responsibility. It is not your place. But if you are the employer, you must assume all responsibility. Never shun your work or place others in charge of it. You are to do your work. If an employer is not good, the work is not good, and all who work under this person fear and neglect their souls. All involved will have to answer for this. The employer will be considered a pariah.

In no way seek the top of the heap or your life will be recycled, and you will not be open to all that is. We seek to change the minds and hearts of those who are in charge of others in the workplace. We seek out those who are dissatisfied with how things are and wish to change the format. We cannot find many, but there are a few. We will now tell you how to change your work so you can ascend.

If the work you must supervise is too complicated, you have to work it out—not your employees. If you do not work it out and others do, you are not working. This is the purpose of work: You are to work every day. So why are you there, if not to do your job? Once you begin to realize supervision of others is the most difficult of all jobs, you are prepared to learn how to do it. If you are lost in the perks of such positions, you will never be free. If you cannot resist the temptation to abuse power, you will be here for many more lifetimes. This cannot be, since the world is ending, so you will be demoted—and this demotion is far worse than anything you can possibly imagine.

If the work of all is good, and all are sure of the work they do, the work of the manager is easy. If the work is not good, and all do not know what to do, the manager must work to correct it. We see no reason why this job is paid so much more than the work of laborers, but when laborers agree they do not want it, others are paid more to assume responsibility. It is an earth rule—not God's rule.

The day all decide to change a rule, the rule is changed. Even if the rule is not good, you are reluctant to change it. This has resulted in a huge abundance of rules, by-laws, and documents requiring the services of those who cannot do anything else. You must slow the process of enacting rules and laws—let up on the work of the dull and witless. Be careful to legalize only what is now a burden. Do not legalize what is capable of destroying you. If you legalize a drug that has a record of descending souls, you do not see it is you who are debauched—not the endangered souls.

In the work of the world, you are now embroiled in a fight. You do not believe it is necessary to live in cities. You believe it is best to live outside city walls, but you are wrong. People need to live as one in order to learn the lessons of this world. You who live in cities cannot handle the work required, because you have no others to support you, but those living far from the core of the city have no one to support them, either. You need one another.

If you dwell in the city and are unwise, you will not live. If you live in the country and are not a farmer, you are unwise. The city forces you to be wise. This is why we seek you there.

You are not to move to mountaintops and prairies to escape the world. The world is you. *You* are here to change the world. How can you change what you know nothing about? How can you live where there is no one else? The world is not for all, but it is the classroom you chose.

Some of you are so uncomfortable that you seek an out and it is granted, because you can opt to be released from this world. It is often referred to as a *Walk-In*, which means you are not the first to inhabit your body. You are here to complete the assignment of another facet of your spiritual being. You may be a *Walk-In*. It is possible, but you are not to become obsessed by the thought.

If you came to Earth late (as a *Walk-In*), you have little memory of your past, little interest in relatives, and no interest in the means of livelihood pursued by the former self. It is not difficult to do. It requires only that you give up—but do not attempt suicide! You simply ask God to release you from this work. You then can continue the work, but on a different level within this plane, and you do it simultaneously with this life. Once you are free of that life, you go forward.

When the other facet, or facets, of your life work out whatever caused you so much pain that you wished to be taken back, the threads will be rewoven into your life. You do not consciously feel it, but the rip in your *wall of spirit* is then mended. When we refer to a *wall of spirit,* we are not referring to anyone else. We are talking about *you.* You are a wall of vibration and color. You are a rainbow. You do not live in the flesh. You do not see, you feel—you are!

When you render a picture of life, you cannot see all the tears you made, nevertheless it still hurts. You feel it. You sense it is not right. You cry. You express passion. You work on it, but it is not right. This is how the wall acts. You are not here to rip into the wall. You are here to live, grow, and enhance it.

We welcome all who can now understand the wall. If you do not, it will come to you. Once the *wall of spirit* is rent, the only way to repair it is to work on what caused the tear.

We help you explore all relationships that hurt and cause you to explore. If they are not as you wish, we will explore what you dislike; but that does not mean the relationship will be changed. If your work on relationships is lacking and not up to our standards, you are held responsible; but if you are unable to control the needs of those around you—and they can be overwhelming, we contact them. If it becomes necessary to end a relationship, you will be released from any guilt. If you are not having problems—merely seeking a change, you will not be released.

The world has certain rules that are used to control the mores of all living within it, but these are not God's laws. If you divorce, this is not God's law. It is the world's law and not of importance to us—unless you hurt another in the process or it is important to the procedures of the next plane. You will have to make considerable allowance for this if you are guilty of harming a child or spouse during the process of divorce. You will not be considered to be worthy of the next plane then. You must begin to make restitution now. Only if such harm is erased while you are here on Earth will you be able to advance. It is a real concern now, since so many have been divorced.

Once you are free of constraint, you must live as a free being. You must not let the rules of man confine your spirit. You must change all laws that bind. You must cease to pander to the words and fears of the media—which you create. You are totally responsible for all words on the air. The air transmits only your thoughts. If you do not agree, you must not transmit. Shut down those airways. Let no one repeat the words. Jam it if necessary, but stop them. You are in charge of your world—not God. God has no interest in why you are not ready to go to the next plane. It is your problem.

If the work of the world is deep in depression, why do you all spend so much money? If you cannot afford to buy, why do you all buy? We see most stores do not offer goods made with your hands. You must seek out special people to do that. Why? If the goods of your hands are not in the marketplace, where will they be sold? You must challenge the large purveyors of goods to handle your work. You must change your methods of buying. You must seek work from the hands of those who work by hand or help support them. They are the artists of your world. If you do not support artists, your work is diminished as well.

You say you are never too rich. We disagree. We seek not the wealth of people—we seek their wisdom. You are not rich, but you can read. You cannot spend money to pay another to read for you. You would not know if they were reading what you want them to read. This is often how the rich are: They pay for services not performed. The lesser in wealth often refer to such people as not having sense—which is often true.

You must seek out wisdom—not wealth. Wealth is no barrier to being able to ascend—it just makes it more difficult. The burdens of wealth are such that occupants often believe only in self. Their descendants cannot free their minds of guilt or lack of work; therefore, they are not wise enough to enlarge the fortune given to them. The wealth of a man is not his money, but his descendents. If this is not true, then why are you here? You are not money. Money is not the same everywhere, but people are.

When the work of the world is done, your work is unable to go forward. You will be placed on a lower plane. This lower plane is often depicted as having demons, but in reality it is not. Demons do not exist—except in your mind. None of us has ever seen a demon. You imagine such things in order to scare yourself into the right path. We disagree with that concept. Please remove such frightening images—we much prefer beauty.

If you are removed to a lower plane, you do not have much trouble ascending again. It is a relatively short lifespan, but it sets your soul back. Why do that? You are not to be a tree or a dog or a cat or any other living organism that exists on Earth, you are the way you are, but in a different form. That form may not be represented on Earth, but you know it. It is not pleasant, and you do not want to repeat it. If you murder someone and are not repentant, you will be dropped to that level to learn. If you commit suicide, it is often that fate, too. We are not free to discuss this.

In this session we are covering many of the loose ends you have brought forward as you read. If you have further questions, this is the appropriate time to call on your Spiritual Guides and ask for their assistance. Remember when calling your Guides—ask aloud. Seek only help you need. Do not ask about others.

Your Guides are your Guides—not the Guides of others. If you ask for help in getting along with others, it takes time. You are to clarify all issues that concern you and ask if the path you choose is right for you. If you are on the right path, often nothing is heard. But if you are on the wrong path, nothing functions properly. We will review it once again before this work is done.

Now we go into the world to observe and ask many more questions. You are a fascinating race. You do not know how much you interest us; however, you are not interesting to many others. We are teachers, so we are interested in how you learn your lessons. We are also concerned about those who are not in school. If you can lead a soul to know God, you are blessed.

We will return with new insights and help. You will be able

to do all the work. You are not the only ones not helping to clear the Earth of its toxins, but you are the only ones who put them there. This is a universal burden on all your souls. We will work to see what each individual can do to relieve this sin from his or her work. It is a sin if you break one of God's rules, and you all have. You must not destroy the home of another. That is not your law—it is God's law. We will come back to this subject in our next session. Today is the best time to review all that was given on the subject of Spiritual Guides. You can review and assimilate it now.

Within a short time the world will be free of such evil things as torture and maiming for wealth, but torture and maiming of souls will continue. You must not permit it to flourish. This is our last word.

Chapter Twenty-Two

In the event we are unable to complete our assignment, we will be upset knowing you could have had an easy life, but chose to make it difficult. It is never the desire or will of God that man have a difficult life. That is a blasphemy often heard, but only from Earth. We abhor any such words and are not pleased.

If your life is difficult, you must analyze it and discover the reason why you are afraid to prosper. If your world is not how you want it, you can always change it. It is mutable and never solid.

When the world was created, God stepped in and changed a few things, but not humans. The weather was not as nice as it is now; it was too hot or so cold many froze to death. So if you think God is not powerful, just wait!

In the beginning of your world—not Earth, but your world—the work of man was simple. You chose to completely intensify the work and alter its structure in order to provide employment for many thousands of people, but now you are more intensely competitive on an individual level and require your own separate arena to prove to yourselves that you are competent.

We seek those who are alone, but not competitive. Competition is a killer! It is not the way to produce the best. It is the way to increase the pressure and stress, but not the goals and good of the individuals involved. You must forego stress, if you are to be free. Freedom from stress and strain is the critical point. If you can do this, you can do almost anything psychically and spiritually. It is the foundation upon which telepathy and clairvoyance are based.

Telepathy is not a *gift*. It is the ability to sense the other person's feelings and see them. You all can do this, and at some time, you have, but clairvoyance is different. It is described as the ability to see at a distance, but it is a *gift*. Only those pleasing to God can discern the truth. All others are unable to simply sense and know what is right or in the heart of others. You may learn clairvoyant skills, but it does not come together properly unless your heart is clearly well, with no evil intentions to use such a gift against others.

For those who experience clairvoyant episodes, you may relax. This is a clear sign you are on the right track. It is not the way for us to say you will automatically advance to the next plane, but it is most probable, as long as you manifest clairvoyant skill.

If you wish to develop that ability, you must meditate and visualize, but it does not necessarily happen. That is the *gift*. Once you can meditate for a good length of time and can visualize the goals you wish to achieve (these two are the components of clairvoyance), you do not automatically produce the ability to see at a distance.

Some are determined to produce visions and travel, and

dedicate a lot of energy to Spirit, but it is the intent that counts most. You must produce a work that demonstrates your moral and theological bent. Once this is done, the work is evaluated and deemed to be worthy or unworthy of spiritual advancement.

If you are ready, the *gift* is offered. You often refer to it as *receiving the call*. We are not calling you. We are offering you a *gift*. If you wish to accept it, it is yours. But if you choose to ignore it, we give it to another. You do not have to accept a gift since it entails a certain degree of obligation and must be respected, but if you do, your life is changed. You are honored for accepting it and you are given further opportunities to earn honors. These honors are normally in the form of *psychic gifts*, but may also be material wealth. You are to be upheld by the world, not played down or put upon or ignored. If the world does not recognize you, we do. That is fair. If you do not deserve the *gift*, you will not receive *the call*. Once you are given a *gift*, treat it always with respect and use it to help yourself and others. You are to be clothed, fed, and sheltered all your life, but you do not have to work on *a gift*.

The work of this world is not the same. It does not guarantee a thing. It is elusive, often painful, and seldom pays; but if you could change your life, would you? To change the world in which you live would require cooperative efforts of all people— and that is unlikely.

We see only disinterest and negativity whenever the subject of environmental pacts and peace are discussed. We see no real changes. The air continues to grow thinner and thinner, and the lack of oxygen is already killing people, but not one organization has made a difference.

If you had a life to give, would you give it? Many of you did that when you came to Earth. You said you would help clear the air and water in order to preserve the planet, but not one of you has made any real commitment to the cause yet. Where are all of you? Why are you waiting?

We are here to rouse you from your sleep!

In the work of this world there is a lot of worry and fright. You do not like your work, yet you all continue to fight for it. You seek employment. You beg for jobs. You humble yourself to man, but not to God. You ask for help, but not one of the jobs you get is for *you*. Work today is demeaning! You are expected to give up your life for the establishment of a business that does not care if you die. You cannot work even when hired to do it, because of political repercussions if you do so.

In many countries unions and companies work hand-in-hand to submerge the issues of the worker, but in America this does not exist. In America, unions request help to settle disputes, but do not call upon God. They ask management for what they should seek from God. Unions themselves condemn individuals who work hard. They seek out over-producers (or whatever you call them) and chastise them for breaking rank. We do not care for this. This is why unions are being punished now.

Man is never to be without work, but today people do not

realize they are responsible for it—not an employer. If you constantly find yourself out of work, go into your heart and seek out the reason. If it is you, change the work. If it is the work, change you. This is not backward or stupid. You need to analyze yourself, and then produce the best that is within you.

Wherever the world is wrong, God is blamed. But if you are God and God is everywhere, why is the world wrong? Whenever you are angry or grief-stricken, you blame God. Why? God does not promise humans everlasting life on Earth. It is a classroom. You must advance or be held over. That is why you return and return to Earth.

We are not here to explain the works of God, but you are. You are expected to understand the inner workings of this planet, its people, its environment, and its atmosphere, but most of you are unable to explain anything about it—even why you are here. That is the worst thing!

We are here for a very short time, and we are not coming back, but you are here for a lifetime and will be returned if you do not learn. So why are you so slow to pick up this message? Why do you still sit and read as though it is all new and incomprehensible? It is clear and easily assimilated, but you block it. We can see you. You cannot fool those above you. It is not unlike anything else where you are subordinate to others.

Now that the work of God is not a mystery (that is true), we seek to help you understand. It is easy to learn facts, but it is difficult to understand why. If you can learn, you can understand. If your life is difficult and does not please you,

you are the only one who can change it. You are not chained to Earth or to a job or family—that comes from your mind. The conscious mind is a jailer. It prevents many of you from achieving your goals. It is ego and not *you*.

When we speak of *ego* we refer to you in the flesh. We are not using it in a psychological sense, rather as a name for that part of *you* that interacts with others on Earth. You are ego. You cannot be You, if you are ego. In the next session we will talk more about the ways ego chains you to your earthly paradise.

Whatever you do and wherever you do it, God is there, but does not intrude. You have *free will* to do whatever you wish. It is your choice to not use your abilities and gifts. You are the only one preventing you from doing so.

We are not here to help you explore the issue of family and friends, and why they are now in this life, but they are here because you want them. You provide the catalyst or not for the formation of a family. Once you decide to have a child, you are involved with the concept until the day you die. You are never relieved of it. However, you are not required to support a child once he or she grows to the age when adulthood should begin—and this age now grows older and older, which is not conducive to maturity.

The earlier a person is considered to be an adult, the more mature that person will be. If your life is not at all like you want to see it, then it is your duty to change. No one else is to change you! Your own mother is unable to change you once you are out of diapers, so how can you change another? You will see that life is full of surprises, and this book contains more than a few of them.

At the end of life you are not alone. Angels often arrive to comfort and warm you, or beg you to leave, but your Guides are still there. They are always there, regardless of whether or not angels arrive. We will not be there. We do not have a part to play then, but You do.

In the final days of a life on Earth, the world is dead to that individual. Regardless of when your death occurs, you will know at the core of your being that the time has arrived, but you may prolong it. However, you should not shorten your life.

If you could end the life of another, would you? We ask that because we see many thinking of killing another, and many do. We are not into your moral code, but your laws are unable to condemn anyone for killing another. That must be changed! You must not let one human being kill another intentionally and receive no punishment. It is not right! We are adamant on that point.

We see no way you can avoid resolving that issue. The world is too soft on criminals now. The age of work is gone, and the world is letting thieves carry off all it produced in the past. The thief is not worthy of such goods and must be treated with contempt. No one is to steal from another. The punishment is eternal condemnation if the thief is not convinced of his misdeed.

The Earth is being stolen from you—and none of you protest, which is why thievery is condoned. When the Earth is destroyed and unable to refuel its jet stream, where will you go? What will you do? Where are you to seek refuge? These are serious questions that require planning. You must think about it or begin to prepare to advance to the next plane. You have no other recourse.

While many play around with environmental issues in order to gratify infantile needs, Earth is gradually deteriorating and unable to refurbish itself. We ask you to begin now to take emergency measures. If you cannot, then let others do it.

You cannot sit alone on Earth. Others are here, too. If many more are born, and those returning are many, Earth will go down in a burst of wasted energy. The death of Earth is not a pleasant thought, but it must be continually thought about if you are all to pull together and save it. The work of your hands has destroyed it—not those who share the planet with you.

We are now aware of a growing interest in *extraterrestrial beings*. We cannot explain much at this time, since our lesson is not on this subject, but we will say this: The *extraterrestrials* you see are not extraterrestrials. They live on Earth, too. You share the same space with beings who do not look like you or act like you, but are just as curious as you are. You do not feel them around you, but you obstruct their progress now. They have lodged many complaints against you and are now being considered for advanced levels of soul development, but you are not.

Any soul that injures another intentionally is unwelcome on the next level of that plane—and certainly cannot advance to the next plane. So if you are contemplating the ignorant tribal warfare of your world of work and society, think better of it and drop it. You will not be able to think on it much longer. Soon your life is not your own.

◈

When your mind catches on an idea, You generate a spark

That sentence sparks. You cannot forget it. It is there. It stands out from the rest of the page and haunts you long after you finish reading this book, because it is true and you know it.

That is why you grow angry and/or anxious. Anger and anxiety are two approaches to fear—neither is good for you. You are unable to cope if you are filled with fear. The fear of Earth being destroyed is not as likely as the work of your hands not being acceptable at the end of your life on Earth. We fear that—not the end of the world.

Your life is not the same as the life of an *extraterrestrial* or animal. You are not the same. You must forget them and dwell on ideals that will elevate *you*. They can live, but you cannot remain on a planet that has little oxygen and lacks good water. You require those two elements. They do not.

When you die or cross over (we prefer the latter term), the work of this world is seen through the eyes of your Guides and related to the Higher Guide who is in the area. This Higher Guide is not attached to a single soul or in charge of that soul's spiritual advancement while on Earth. This Guide is higher by nature of spiritual development on upper planes. This High Guide is a judge of the conditions and failures of the soul. Little escapes this judge, and the verdict may not be pleasing to Spiritual Guides who defend your life at this time.

If the soul's Guides can convince the High Guide of your development, work outstanding may be ignored and you are permitted to advance to the next plane. You are on the highest level of this plane now, so advancement is to the next plane and requires more demanding criteria be passed before promotion. If your Spiritual Guides are unable to convince this High Guide of your ability to distinguish the work of God from man, you can transcend the verdict and appeal once more. We say, once more, because your Spiritual Guides could send you back, thus you meet with the Higher Guide only if you protest this demotion.

The supreme judge is God! You cannot appeal God's decision. The work of this world is not of God, but is God. To ignore this is to confirm a seat on the life train moving nowhere. To dream of this train is a reminder that you are not going anywhere and must get off the train at the next station to check your destination. You are off the train now. Let us hope your destination is clear.

If this session is too disquieting, your mind will blur and erase every area you fear, but it does not change the truth. You will read it again and learn from it at another time, hopefully, before you cross over.

Chapter Twenty-Three

In the work of this world, you are the only one responsible for doing it; but in the work of the next world, you are not. You are only a part of your entire being. You are a multi-faceted being who is not only capable of further development, but will do so.

The end of this world is not the end of *THE WORLD*. The work of God is not the only work to be changed. Your work is to be changed and modified, too. You are not ready if your work cannot be challenged. The end product of all work is the ability to sell it. If you cannot sell your life's work, you are stuck with it.

We see you are confused. This is not easy to dictate. The Scribe, unlike the majority of readers of this book, is incapable of necessary bluntness; however, you are. If the Scribe could tell you everything she had to do, you would not be pleased. If you were to tell us all you had to do, we would not be pleased. The life you live is different, and the life from which you spring is not alike, but your future is similar.

You are not to be the only ones promoted to the next plane. Many beings exist who are not like you, but similar. In the next plane you all look the same, but are not. In this plane you all look different, but are the same. The differences on this plane are more cosmetic than actual, but differences on the next plane reflect lives lived on this one and, therefore, are totally different.

We seek those who are the same as *The Scribe*. We do not seek boasters. We do not condemn them, but we are not interested. The world is full of boasters and braggarts. What the world needs is the meek and the mild.

If you could, would you change? It is unlikely any of you could change even if you wanted to change, yet we seek those who do. You can be forced to live through difficult times. It is your choice if it is difficult or easy. You are the decision maker. Your Guides will always avoid the especially difficult passages you are prone to take, but they will follow if you insist. It is much easier to ask their advice *before* you start a new venture; however, that is not easy for most of you to do, because you do not believe in God.

That seems to shock you, but what else can explain such behavior? You live wantonly and cannot condemn evil. You look at the evil around you and apologize for it. You never worry about the victim. You fight to control punishment to the evildoer. So who is evil? Evil is a word seldom heard on Earth, yet it exists everywhere. By denying it exists, do you believe it does not exist?

We seldom ask questions of our students on upper planes, but you do not think enough, so we ask. If you do not know why, you must sit down and determine the reason you refuse to question your society. Do you have any way to input ideas and dreams? Do you get satisfaction from your work? Is the life you live one of graciousness and fine works of art? Are you the real *you*? Do you seek the best? What of the work you do— Is it the best you can do? Do you enjoy it? Are you sincere?

When the world is void of harmony and justice, we see no reason to want to remain, but you do. Why? If the world is unfair, why do you stay?

Your work is done!

You are not the average person if you read this book continuously from the beginning to this point. You are not the only one, but *you* are special to us. You are different. Do you not feel it? Do you not see it? We do. You are the type to change the world!

The herd of people disinterested in their spiritual development will never change this world. They like it as it is. It is their work. They are unconcerned about you. You are of no interest to them.

We send *you* the work of God. If you are interested in doing your share, please answer. If not, do not hesitate to leave. It is your life. You do not have to work. You do not have to socialize and learn to tolerate all other humans—and may harm anyone you please, but you will not leave Earth if you do.

If your life is different from what it was when you began to read this book, we are thrilled. If you feel a difference, you are different. It is the way of God. First you feel—then you see.

We are here to help and guide you—and your Spiritual Guides. We are not here to direct your work. If you wish to remain, you may do so. If you wish to leave, you need only work hard every day of your life on something that pleases *you* and mankind—not the work of selfish ends. You also have to go out into the world and meet others and enjoy them. You may not harbor resentments and bear malice towards others. You are not to be intolerant. You are to let others enjoy themselves. If you do not, you are not free of prejudice.

We are aware these two areas are the most likely to hold you back. That is why we stress them, but the third requirement— *You must not harm any other human*—is the worst sin.

If you hurt another person, you cannot erase this stain. It is a blot on you and your aura. It stands out. It is not easy to explain. It requires a tribute. If you paid the price here on Earth for such malice, you do not need to fear later. If you are free and society is unwilling to notice, or you can hide it, you will pay later. It is the balance of justice. No one can escape it.

What happens to those who cannot escape the world? You are not alone here, and you are not the only ones to live on Earth. If Earth is destroyed, all suffer; but if only the air and water are destroyed, only humans will suffer. We now sense this is what will happen, but we are not privy to God's plans. You will know if you continue to return to Earth.

Some of you are still struggling with the concept of

reincarnation. It is not easy to understand why, but we will try once again to reinvent that wheel so you may understand it now. Many words have been channeled on this subject already, but some remain ignorant.

When you exist in the flesh, you also exist in other dimensions. You are not the only beings of your soul. You exist in another time and place. You are multi-dimensional—not three-dimensional, as seen on Earth. However, you are unlike the Earthly entity. You are an electrical impulse. You cannot be directed. You direct your own destiny. If you decide as an entity to ignore the work of man, it is your right; and if you decide to investigate such work, you can.

Many souls choose to explore the negativity of this planet and seek the expression of human bodies. It is a different experience and not very pleasant, but there are many good reasons for doing so. One is you can realize the difficulty of manifesting thought. It takes many months (even years) on Earth to manifest a thought into being, but on other planes what you think is created instantly.

This experience gives the entity a fear of doing too much. It is a humbling experience. The power is slowed and channeled into many different extremes—many are unpleasant, but the main reason you come to Earth is to learn tolerance and patience. These are virtues to be cultivated here.

When life is over on your plane, you can advance; but many completely absorb the negative energy and become wise to the ways of this world and decide to renege and stay here. It is unwise, but many do it. Once you learn all there is to learn on Earth, you should quickly leave. It is not wise to stay!

Wherever life takes you, you are still in God, but God is not in your work. Your work is *you*. You bring that work to God; and if it is pleasing, you are rewarded. Your *gift* is one of spiritual blessing, not money or its equivalent. Fame is this world's blessing and curse, but not God's. Know the difference!

Wherever you take your life, God is there, but God does not take you there. You are expected to do all you can to improve this work, not destroy or impair it. If you have done enough work to improve the world, you may be excused from it. If your work in the world is not done, you will be expected to finish it—even if it takes forever.

The reason there are so many on Earth now is that God is moving to change it. If all of you do not get off Earth, Earth is going to begin to change. God is not in the world, but is in Earth.

We are not of Earth, but we are of this world. We have been here. We once experienced a life here and have been sent to redeem it, but we are not of the world you live in now. This is much worth your figuring it out. If you can, you will be ready for the next riddle.

When the world is closed to the next one, what will happen? We see you never contemplated it could happen. Well, it is. You will be unable to advance directly to the next plane much longer. The gates of heaven (as you so often describe it) are swinging closed. The narrow way is suddenly closer and not as likely to remain open. If you are caught, you cannot escape. You will be condemned to this planet—and this planet is condemned.

When the world you know is over, who is in charge? Angels! You are to be escorted to the next plane, if you meet the criteria; if you do not, you will be ending your time on nether planes. These planes are not as pleasant as Earth. You have been there and did not remain. You often fled from them, but you will be returned until another experience such as life on Earth can be described and manifested. The others will go before you.

Without a care, that is how life on Earth is supposed to be, but most of you are worried. You worry over trivial matters that are of no use to anyone, and you care not for the major issues that are killing you. If this is the description of your life, you are unable to care. You cannot clear your mind to meditate. You will never hear God.

It is not wise to be unable to hear God. If God asks for help, how can you respond if you cannot hear? We expect an answer. If the answer is not positive, you need to humbly beg of You and God pardon for all your sins, and immediately begin to pray and meditate. If you do not worry, we will help you listen ever more intently to the words of God. This is our promise.

In the last days of your life on Earth, you will be asked to begin a new life. It is not a rhetorical question. You are asked to begin again, but you may instead come back to Earth again. This time please ask to be moved to the next plane. We urge you to do this! However, in the end it is your choice.

In the work of this plane are many ways to be humble, but few of you are. The work of this planet is not as easy as it is on other planes, but not as satisfying either. It is unlike anything anywhere else. Everyone on upper planes is constantly concerned about *you*. You are a worry of sorts to them. If you leave, you will free them to do other things.

Many humans constantly call angels to do their work—which is obviously not the way God helps humans. Humans are in power here. You can be whatever you wish in this life, and can choose the design of your life. If you wish to change your life, change yourself—you are the designer.

Do not call angels! Angels are often called by Spiritual Guides, but *you* are not to do it while here. Ask your Guides for help! If it is appropriate and within the realm of angels, they will come to you. Do not call them! This is blasphemy. God has charge over them—not you.

If you call angels and archangels to you, you are indeed in the deepest trouble of your life. Your Guides are here, too. They seek out angels and tell of your troubles. You never need do it. All of life is difficult if you have no faith, but life is great if you are faithful to God.

This is the way of man ~
To fear God, but not obey

Whatever you decide, it is your decision. You may come back to Earth—or you may not. It is your decision. God is not trying to move you. You are not of such importance that God will change the way the world exists in order to spare you. You are of the world or you are of God. Again, this may appear contradictory, but it is not.

You chose to come to Earth. You chose this life. You chose to live this life as you do now. You are responsible for those choices. You could have chosen a different existence. God grants you the choice, but you are responsible for the outcome. To be responsible means you learn and accept what happens.

When the work of God is done, all know it!
God does not ask for feedback, and
God does not ask you for payment

You are to leave this life and advance to the next plane. If you decide to return to Earth again, it is not the work of God. God stepped in at this time to warn all who fear, but those who do not are permitted to return. You are not fearful. You are strong. If you can, tell those who need to know, but never push anyone to accept.

In the work of God is the work of man, but much of the work of man is not reflective of God. This is the beginning of the end for any race. If you no longer respect God, you will not long respect man, either. This disrespect reflects upon you—not God.

You are the human you chose to be. You are not the human

God made, if you chose to destroy the tissue. The tissue from which you are made is meant to last as long as the Spirit within wishes to remain on Earth, which may be long or short. If your decision to leave Earth is premature, you linger long in flesh. If your decision to leave Earth is postponed beyond the length of time you originally intended to live, your body becomes frail but continues. If your body is strong at the time of crossing over, you judged your life well. These are simple thoughts, but deep.

If you doubt the wisdom, because the words are not complex, you are simple. Your life is not to be judged by the standards of this world, but by the simple laws of God. If you are simple, you make things complex. If you are wise, you keep it simple.

When the time to cross over arrives and you are unafraid, we will never ask you *when* you decided, but *if* you decided. If you say you decided, then your life is good and well and you are ready to progress to the next plane. But if the decision is not made and you are confused about why you were on Earth and what you should have done while here, we will recommend that you return. It is your decision. Whatever you do, it is always your decision. Even if you make no actual statement or deed, it is a decision.

All who do nothing to return the Earth to its original state are stating you want it this way. If you wanted it different, you would be working on changing it right now. We are not haranguing you or nagging, we are repeating the message for the slow learners.

The role of the teacher is important, but it is the student who determines how good the teacher is. Many children are being neglected by their teachers at home and elsewhere. You may see others as teachers, but not yourself—*you are all teachers*. It is your decision whether or not you do a good job. Ask your students if you do your job. Ask for the opinion of your best friend. Do you have a good friend?

These are the ways of the world. You are of the world now, but not forever. In the end all is known. You are the work of God, now do the work of God and have no regrets.

We are here for all who need to begin the search for the right way. We are here to put you on the right track if you have strayed, but we are not here to take you to the other side. That is the role of your Spiritual Guides.

If you have learned nothing else from this literature, we will have accomplished much if you are now aware of the presence of Spiritual Guides and know they are commissioned to be with you all your life. You can never say you were alone, because you are not. You have Guides! We will leave—but not your Guides.

It is a matter of some concern to all of us, but it is time to leave this matter in your hands. You are to contact us if we can be of service or help you understand this work, but you are on your own. Only your Spiritual Guides can intrude into your life—or one of God's angels may, but we can only teach if you ask for us.

This is the end of our work. We will search for those who are here to help us. We will contact men, but few will give of themselves. That is the way. You are not obligated. You are free.

Be Sure to Also Read...

The Teachers of the Higher Planes
The Work Begins
Ruth Lee, *Scribe*

Second in *The Books of Wisdom* series scribed by Ruth Lee, **The Work Begins** takes over where **We Are Here** ends. *The Teachers of the Higher Planes* continue to help mankind develop and improve our lives in this space and time.

According to *The Teachers*, we arrive on Earth blessed with inner wisdom and enough knowledge to pass the tests of this existence—then return to our ultimate spiritual source. Are you ready?

The Work Begins teaches you how to work with Spirit and enjoy life while here, regardless of your past. To change your mind or enter higher levels of knowledge entails acceptance that work is required. If you are not using your source of inner wisdom, you need to read this book!

To read more about

The Work Begins
Visit: www.LeeWayPublishing.com